GW00514722

Business Angels

Business Angels

Securing Start Up Finance

Patrick Coveney
Karl Moore

John Wiley & Sons
Chichester · New York · Weinheim · Brisbane · Singapore · Toronto

National   01243 779777
International   (+44) 1243 779777
e-mail (for orders and customer service enquiries):
cs-books@wiley.co.uk
Visit our Home Page on http://www.wiley.co.uk
or http://www.wiley.com

Other Wiley Editorial Offices

John Wiley & Sons, Inc., 605 Third Avenue,
New York, NY 10158-0012, USA

WILEY-VCH Verlag GmbH, Pappelallee 3,
D-69469 Weinheim, Germany

Jacaranda Wiley Ltd, 33 Park Road, Milton,
Queensland 4064, Australia

John Wiley & Sons (Asia) Pte Ltd, 2 Clementi Loop #02-01,
Jin Xing Distripark, Singapore 129809

John Wiley & Sons (Canada) Ltd, 22 Worcester Road,
Rexdale, Ontario M9W 1L1, Canada

Library of Congress Cataloging-in-Publication Data

Coveney, P.
    Business angels : securing start up finance /
Patrick Coveney and Karl Moore.
        p.   cm.
    Includes bibliographical references and index.
    ISBN 0-471-97718-7
    1. Angels (Investors)—Great Britain.   2. New business
enterprises—Great Britain—Finance.   3. Venture capital—Great
Britain.   I. Coveney, Patrick.   II. Title.
HG4027.6.M66   1998
658.15'224'0941—dc21   97–31197
                                                                              CIP

British Library Cataloguing in Publication Data

A catalogue record for this book is available from the British Library

ISBN 0-471-97718-7

Typeset in 10/12pt Times by Dorwyn Ltd, Rowlands Castle, Hants
Printed and bound in Great Britain by Bookcraft (Bath) Ltd., Midsomer Norton, Somerset
This book is printed on acid-free paper responsibly manufactured from sustainable forestry, in which at least two trees are planted for each one used for paper production.

Contents

PART IV   WHERE ANGELS TREAD

For Karl this book is dedicated to his wife Brigitte
and son, Erik

For Patrick this book is dedicated to Hugh
and Pauline, for their fantastic support
for many years

Acknowledgements

The authors would like to thank Mark van Osnabrugge for his many weeks of hard work on this book. In addition to conducting background research for the authors, he was very helpful in writing three chapters. His detailed knowledge of the area and high quality of work were most valuable. We are grateful that he took time away from research and teaching commitments to help us finish the book.

Mark is currently in the last year of his doctoral degree (D.Phil.) at Oxford University, analysing the investment attractions and behaviours of Business Angels and venture capitalists. Mark is the second doctoral student at Oxford within the last two years (in addition to one of the book's authors) to conduct research on Business Angels.

Thus far, Mark has collected data on 262 investments that have been made in early stage firms in the UK over the last two years and has almost finished analysing the data. His results are already very promising and will certainly shed more light on some previously under-studied areas of Business Angel research. His work builds on some of the research presented in this book and will hopefully be another step towards a deeper understanding of Business Angels and venture capitalists.

The authors would also like to thank a number of other people without whom this book could never have been researched or written. Hamish Stevenson and Janine Nahapiet were instrumental in structuring the initial research and interpreting the findings. They both invested significant time and energy in the project and their practical guidance was greatly appreciated by both authors. Without the support of Venture Capital Report this project could not have been completed; we are indebted to Lucius, James and especially Dave Amis for their help. Finally, we would like to thank the 500 Angel investors who participated in our research. All our insights are grounded in their experiences.

PART I
Who Needs an Angel?

1
Introduction

An increasing number of Britons are starting or considering starting their own businesses. For some people a small business represents the opportunity for an extra bit of income; for others it represents the opportunity to combine parenthood with part-time activities; and for the many middle managers who have been made redundant by giant corporations or the public sector it represents a better future. Whatever your reasons, we have written this book to help guide you through an important part of getting your business on its feet—raising the money necessary to fund its early stages.

A typical entrepreneur starts off by using savings or perhaps taking out a second mortgage, then borrows from friends and family; at a certain point these sources dry up, even as the new venture takes off. When a small firm becomes successful and has a track record venture capital firms and banks will consider funding its future. However, between the friends/family and venture capital firms/banks lies what we call the "equity gap" or "chasm". Figure 1.1 shows the equity gap, probably the single biggest hurdle for entrepreneurs. The overwhelming challenge of bridging the gap is among the top reasons for small businesses not achieving their full potential. The way many successful entrepreneurs bridge this gap is through a source of funding called Business Angels—that is, informal suppliers of risk capital.

From research we have undertaken at Oxford University we have gathered a considerable amount of practical information to help you understand Business Angels and how to increase your chance of success of obtaining funding from them. We hope you enjoy this book and, more importantly, find it useful for your small business.

As well as looking at Business Angels in detail and explaining how you can find them, we outline what *they* are looking for and how best you can present your case to them. We explain what happens once an investor has expressed interest in your venture and what you can expect from them.

Figure 1.1 The Equity Gap

STARTING YOUR VENTURE

You are not alone in wanting to start your own business. Small entrepreneurial ventures are playing an increasingly important role in the UK
economy. Research suggests that in the period 1982–1991 firms with fewer
than 20 employees created nearly two and a half million jobs, whereas larger
firms actually reduced their number of jobs by a quarter of a million during
that time. Many small firms expand rapidly and create substantial employment. David Storey of Warwick University's Business School contends that
over the course of a decade 4 per cent of the businesses that start up will
produce 50 per cent of the jobs created.

A critical issue for vibrant young businesses is finding sufficient funding for
start-up and growth. Most entrepreneurs first look to the formal sector: banks,
the stock market and venture capitalists. These sources, however, can fund
only a small percentage of the many ventures that turn to them. Most successful start-up ventures find their funds in an area of the economy that is less well
known, the informal venture capital sector. This book details the informal
venture capital sector because it is the most attractive source of funds and

offers critical management help to most entrepreneurs. At the heart of this book is a new way of understanding these "Business Angels".

Business Angels have tended to be regarded as if they were all exactly the same. In this book we outline six types of Angels. By understanding the different types an entrepreneur can better decide which is the best for their venture and more fruitfully focus their efforts in locating the "right" Angel. The categorisation of Angels we have developed is based on a major long-term research project we undertook at Oxford University. This looked at the activities of nearly 500 active and potential informal investors and analysed the specific details of 467 investment deals. Though the ideas we present here are research based, we have tried to write a practical and useful book. Throughout, we suggest practical ways that entrepreneurs can successfully raise funds for their start-up ventures and gain the most from their dealings with business investors.

In the next section we discuss the principal alternative sources of funds available to entrepreneurs. We then focus on the sector that research suggests is the most useful to entrepreneurs—the informal venture capital. This chapter provides a quick overview and following chapters will cover each subject, including the different phases of equity financing and how to choose an Angel, with a chapter on each type of Angel.

SOURCES OF FUNDS FOR START-UP VENTURES

Once entrepreneurs have exceeded the limit of their own supplies of funds (including those of family and friends etc.), there are three principal external sources of funding available to them:

1. formal sources such as banks
2. venture capital companies
3. informal investors, often referred to as Business Angels.

Two of these sources, banks and venture capital companies, have moved away from providing external finance to entrepreneurs. The first part of this section looks at this finance gap. We will also look at banks and venture capital companies and attempt to explain why these organisations have reduced their levels of investment in new and growing businesses.

THE FINANCE GAP FOR NEW AND GROWING BUSINESSES

This is not a new problem in the UK—as far back as 1931 the Macmillan Committee recognised the problem when they talked about an "equity financing gap" between the needs of individual entrepreneurs seeking capital and the requirements of the institutions formally supplying it. In particular it maintained that there was a finance gap for firms that were too big to be financed solely by banks and too small to interest the formal stock market. Forty years later the problem still existed according to the 1971 Bolton Report, which looked more specifically at British entrepreneurs and venture capital funds and recognised an equity gap between the needs of entrepreneurs and the requirements of investors.

In 1988 the Confederation of British Industry (CBI) conducted a survey and found that companies had great difficulty raising loan and equity finance for amounts less than £250 000. They followed up this research with another study of British small and medium-sized enterprises in 1992 and again found that these firms had great difficulty locating loan and equity capital in the £50 000 to £500 000 range. In 1993 the CBI concluded that for various reasons banks and venture capital companies were not interested in making this form of investment (later sections of this book will review some of these reasons).

Some analysts (e.g. Mason and Harrison, 1991) suggest that the small firm finance gap is a function of both demand and supply factors. They contend that the finance gap is primarily a supply-side shortage of seed, start-up and early stage finance and suggest that both banks and venture capital funds have moved away from making these types of investment. However, they also point to demand-side problems and suggest that many entrepreneurs do not actively seek equity financing packages. In fact, Mason and Harrison believe that many small firms consider equity financing only as a last resort because they do not want to hand over control and independence to the new investors.

Furthermore, when entrepreneurs do look for this form of finance, they often make unrealistic demands on their investors. David Smith (1994) writing in *Management Today* pointed out that many owner/managers of smaller firms are by nature extremely independent and as such are often unwilling to give up any control of their ventures to outside investors. He suggests, however, that the optimum solution to their financing problem may well involve having to give up a degree of that independence.

PROBLEMS WITH BANK FINANCE FOR NEW AND GROWING BUSINESSES

Retail, or high street, banks still represent a major source of finance for new and growing businesses (see CBI, 1993; Mason and Harrison, 1995), although they have become less willing to lend money to new ventures. Part of the reason for this is that the burden of debt limits the entrepreneur's room to manoeuvre and leaves them badly exposed if trading conditions become difficult.

Recent research (CBI, 1993; Oates, 1992; Mason and Harrison, 1993, 1996) suggests that the major British retail banks have become less willing to finance entrepreneurial ventures with secured loans after their losses in the early 1990s. These banks had been willing to provide high levels of secured credit to finance start-up and expanding small businesses during the macro-economic boom of the mid 1980s, but the recession following this boom led to a significant increase in the rate of failure of these small ventures. Dun and Bradsheet (Bank of England Quarterly Bulletin, February 1994) calculated that through the recession (1991–93) the number of business failures rose to 55 000 a year compared with a more normal rate through the 1980s of fewer than 20 000 a year. The vast majority of these failures occurred in the small business sector and the combined effect of this was to increase greatly the level of bad debts suffered by the high street banks. The strain of these bad debts, with their negative impact on profits, on the overstretched retail banking sector has meant that the banks are now increasingly reluctant to provide loans to all but the most secure business proposals.

Perhaps most importantly, in a 1993 report the CBI suggested that many of the high street banks do not see a role for themselves in providing equity finance to small businesses.[1] Where the banks do choose to provide finance to small businesses, they tend to prefer to use overdraft finance rather than longer-term, fixed-rate, financial packages (for evidence of this, see CBI, 1993; Smith, 1994). Business reporter David Smith (1994) has suggested that banks prefer to provide short-term overdraft packages because they offer the fastest route to reducing exposure to businesses experiencing financial difficulties.

PROBLEMS WITH VENTURE CAPITAL FINANCE FOR NEW AND GROWING BUSINESSES

Although Britain has a venture capital industry that is more developed than any other in Europe, in both size and sophistication, it does not cater properly for high-risk new and young businesses. In fact, most analysts (CBI, 1993; Mason and Harrison, 1991, 1995; Murray, 1994) view the formal venture capital industry as not being a major source of finance for entrepreneurial ventures. Most British venture capital firms have tended to avoid small-scale investments because the administrative headaches are too great when matched against the likely returns. Supplying risk capital to entrepreneurial ventures is simply not attractive to venture capital funds because the fixed "deal costs" have rendered such deals unprofitable, and the potential for earning high fee income on this type of investment is low.

The British Venture Capital Association (BVCA) in a 1994 report found that British venture capital companies invested a total of £1.23 billion in 1066

UK-based companies in 1993. However, only 236 of these investments were in start-up or early-stage businesses. In all this comprised 19 per cent of their investee companies and, more significantly, only 6 per cent of the total funds invested. According to Murray (1994), Smith (1994) and Woolfman (1993), venture capital firms focus more heavily on management buy-outs and the provision of development finance to existing businesses, rather than investing substantial funds in new ventures. This deliberate positioning of the formal venture capital industry away from the smaller end of the risk capital market has led to a gap for small firms in risk capital markets.

INFORMAL SUPPLIERS OF RISK CAPITAL

As we outlined above, the average entrepreneur often encounters difficulties in seeking funds from the formal sector. The solution for many is to turn to informal suppliers of risk capital—Business Angels.

Business Angels are important as a source of risk capital for two main reasons. The first is the growing demand on the part of early stage entrepreneurs for this form of finance. Second, the type of advice that many Business Angels bring to their investments can be invaluable to the success of a fledgling firm. The remainder of this book will focus on Business Angels, and look at who they are and how to approach them to find your venture.

THE RESEARCH BEHIND THIS BOOK

Despite the importance of Business Angels as a source of capital to entrepreneurs, very little large-scale research has been carried out on them. This dearth of academic research, particularly in Britain, has stemmed in part from difficulties in the identification of significant numbers of Angels, and also from the desire of many Angels to protect their privacy. These problems have had serious implications for the approaches used by previous researchers. In fact, the most influential British researchers in this area, Mason and Harrison and their associates (1990–95) base their conclusions around a series of small-scale surveys (each of fewer than 100 investors) and a set of focused case studies.

With the kind support of Venture Capital Report and other business introduction services in Britain, we were able to survey nearly 500 Business Angel investors/potential investors. This book reports on the investment activity, characteristics and preferences of this group. In addition, this project separately profiled 467 actual investment deals, involving a total level of funds of more than £50 million.

TYPES OF ANGELS

Figure 1.2 illustrates the investment activity and characteristics of the four different types of active Angel we have identified. Explanations of all six types of Angel are given below and more detail is given in Part II.

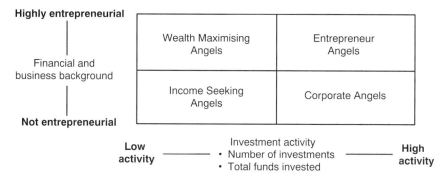

Figure 1.2   The Investment Activity and Characteristics of the Different Angel Types

Entrepreneur Angels

Entrepreneur Angels are the most active and experienced informal investors and as a result represent a particularly appealing source of finance for the first-time entrepreneur. The key points to remember about Entrepreneur Angels are:

- they are individuals who make frequent, large-scale investments in new and growing ventures—they are active and ready to go ahead if you can convince them of the potential of your venture
- they are considerably wealthier than other individual Angel types
- they have been more entrepreneurial in their own business careers
- though they invest principally for financial gain these Angels are also attracted by the fun and satisfaction of making informal investments and often interact a great deal with the founders/managers of their investments—an excellent source of inexpensive management consulting advice.

Corporate Angels

Corporate Angels are companies that make Angel type investments. The key points to remember about Corporate Angels are:

- they have corporate resources at their disposal and were found to invest greater levels of funds than most individual Angel investors
- they invest predominantly for financial gain.

Income Seeking Angels

Income Seeking Angels are active individual investors who have made one or two low-level investments over the past three years. The key points to remember about Income Seeking Angels are:

- they are well-off but not as wealthy as the other Angel types
- they make their investments both for financial gain and to generate a job/income for themselves.

Wealth Maximising Angels

This group of active Angel investors comprise wealthy private individuals who have made several investments in new and growing ventures. The key points to remember about Wealth Maximising Angels are:

- not surprisingly, they tend to be very wealthy, though without being quite as rich as Entrepreneur Angels
- they make their investments primarily for financial gain.

Latent Angels

Latent Angels are inactive Angels who have made one or more informal investments in the past, but who have remained inactive for at least the past three years. The key points to remember about Latent Angels are:

- they are very wealthy, self-made private individuals, with substantial funds available to invest, who are now interested in making informal investments
- of all the Angel types, Latent Angels are the most concerned with venture location
- they cite the lack of suitable locally based proposals as having restricted their investment activity.

Virgin Angels

Virgin Angels are that group of inactive investors who have not yet made an investment in an unquoted venture. Existing American and British research suggests that there are many more Virgin Angels than active Angels.[2] The key points to remember about Virgin Angels are:

- they are private individuals who are looking to provide finance to new or growing businesses, with a view to creating a job or a regular income for themselves, and to earn higher returns than those available on the stock market
- they are not as wealthy as active Business Angels and have fewer funds available to invest
- they do not cite this lack of funds as restricting their investment activity, but instead point to an absence of suitable investment proposals.

FINDING THE ANGEL FOR YOUR VENTURE

From our research we have found that we can usefully divide up Business Angels into the above six types. As we have indicated, each of the types differs from the others on a number of key characteristics. But which Angel is best for you?

Figure 1.3 helps provide direction on how to match your venture and business background with the most appropriate of the six types of Angels. The bottom axis represents your experience—in this case, the number of ventures that you have previously been involved in (including any large firms you have worked for in the same industry as your proposed new venture). The vertical

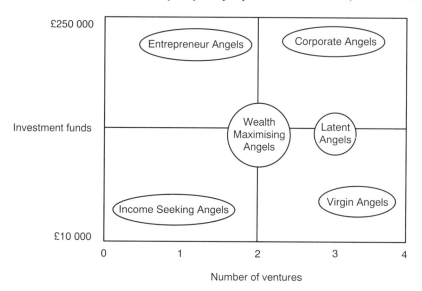

Figure 1.3 Angel Matching

axis gives a range of figures from which to mark the amount of funds you are seeking. The cut-offs are approximate, but provide a useful rule of thumb to help you identify the type of Business Angel that may best be able to help you.

After finding the *two* Angel types that best appear to provide a match with your needs and experience, we suggest that you, at least, read the chapters on those Angels.

SUMMARY

In this chapter we have given an overview of an important source of new venture funding—Business Angels. Our research at Oxford University has revealed six quite different Business Angel types. This chapter provided a thumbnail sketch of each Angel type and a way of matching your experience and required funds with them. The following chapters will cover in more depth each subject touched on in this chapter, from the different phases of equity financing to how to choose an Angel, with a chapter on each type of Angel.

The rest of Part I looks at how to find a Business Angel who can help you, and at a typical informal investment deal. Part II has a chapter on each type of Business Angel, based on information from our research results.

NOTES

1. The British banking experience is mirrored by the American experience. Ennew and Binks (1993) found that American retail banks were not keen to finance entrepreneurial ventures due to losses incurred in this sector in the late 1980s, and their subsequent reappraisal of small business risk. Furthermore several researchers (Ennew and Binks, 1993; Goodman and Allen, 1992; Peek and Rosengren, 1992) have found that where banks do offer to provide this form of finance it is more expensive and comes with greater disclosure requirements than was the case in the 1980s.
2. Sources on this include, Mason and Harrison (1995); Riding *et al* (1993); Wetzel and Freear (1993). For example, Riding *et al* (1993) estimated that there are about 100 000 potential Angels in Canada of which only 3 per cent are currently active. In the British case, Mason and Harrison (1995) claim that if half of the Virgin Angels became active, the total informal venture capital market would grow to ten times the size of formal venture capital market.

2
Locating Business Angels

One of the biggest problems restricting the further growth of the informal venture capital market is the lack of knowledge between entrepreneurs seeking equity finance and investors looking to fund new and early stage businesses. On the one hand it was very clear to us that Business Angels would invest more frequently if they had access to a better range of investment proposals. However, we also found that many potential ventures, which meet the minimum growth and return criteria of Business Angels, still go unfunded. Clearly there are inefficiencies in the information transfer process that mean that the "right" type of Angel is not getting access to proposals for the "right" kind of venture.

This chapter first identifies the principal sources of information for Angels and looks at the problems that Angels can have with these sources. We then look at the type of information Angels require and recommend practical steps that entrepreneurs should take when seeking equity finance from an informal investor. In Britain there are now a number of organisations, referred to as business introduction services, that try to act as marriage bureaux between entrepreneurs seeking capital and interested potential investors. To date these organisations have not really succeeded in overcoming the problem of inefficient information transfer in the informal venture capital market. We believe, however, that there is a role for business introduction services and we recommend specific ways in which these organisations could better serve entrepreneurs and investors. See Section IV for a listing of such services.

SOURCES OF DEAL INFORMATION CURRENTLY USED BY BUSINESS ANGELS

We studied 467 different investment deals and received details on the manner in which the Business Angels sourced these deals. Our research found that friends/family (35 per cent) and business associates (23 per cent) are the most common sources (see Figure 2.1). The fact that these two groups account for 58 per cent of all deals reinforces the findings of some existing British research (Mason and Harrison, 1993; National Westminster Bank, 1993), which found that personal contacts and business acquaintances were the principal information source for Angels, and that business introduction services played a minor role.

We also sought to determine:

- the total number of proposals Business Angels receive ·
- the number of those that were of interest to them
- the number in which they actually offered to invest.

On average, Business Angels receive about 40 investment proposals in a typical year, of which about 20 per cent are of interest to them; they offer to invest in 5 per cent of the total proposals—about a quarter of the "interesting proposals". It is very clear that Angels are being deluged with a large number of unsuitable proposals and as a result reject the vast majority (95 per cent) of them. In fact, it appears that 80 per cent of the proposals they receive are of no interest to them whatsoever. In this regard the findings support the existing research on Business Angels. For instance, Mason and Harrison (1994a)

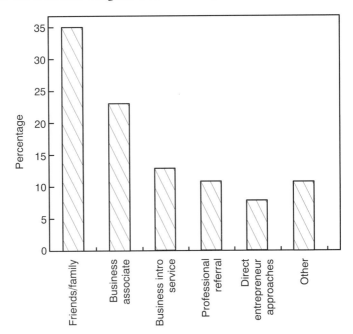

Figure 2.1 Sources of Information for Deals

suggest that Angels reject seven out of every eight proposals they receive. However, the level of acceptance is still slightly higher than that of venture capital companies, which several researchers (Dixon, 1991; Maier and Walker, 1987; Sweeting, 1991) have suggested is typically in the 1–3 per cent range. The key task for the entrepreneur is to target a select number of Angels to whom their project would be of interest. The next section of this chapter provides specific guidelines to help you locate suitable "interested" investors.

There is a widespread perception that Business Angels are dissatisfied with the current information sources available to them (KPMG, 1992; Mason and Harrison, 1993; National Westminster Bank, 1993). Our research confirmed this perception: we found that almost two-thirds of both active and potential Angels would have made a greater number of informal investments in the preceding three years if they had had access to more suitable proposals. Similarly, 70 per cent of the Angels feel that their investment activity is now restricted by a lack of suitable investment opportunities. It is especially unfortunate that Angels are unable to locate suitable proposals because they have considerable resources available for further investment. In fact, 50 per cent of the Angels we surveyed had more than £100 000 available specifically for informal investment. The challenge for entrepreneurs, small businesses and policymakers is to find mechanisms for getting the right proposals on to the desks of the right Angels.

GUIDELINES FOR LOCATING SUITABLE BUSINESS ANGELS

We have identified six distinct types of Angel investor. Entrepreneurs need to be aware that each of these types of Angels have different investment portfolios, come from different financial and business backgrounds, and offer a range of different financial and non-financial benefits to the ventures they support. Entrepreneurs must decide on the most appropriate type of Angel for their venture and deliberately seek to target them. For example, Corporate Angels and Entrepreneur Angels are more likely to seek majority shareholdings than the other Angel types, but will probably offer greater levels of funds. On the other hand, many entrepreneurs are not willing to forgo substantial stakes and may prefer to enter a relationship with one of the other Angel types. Similarly, a first-time entrepreneur may prefer to use an Entrepreneur Angel because of their hands-on experience of entrepreneurship, or an Income Seeking Angel who may take a more active day-to-day involvement in the venture. Alternatively, an experienced entrepreneur may be more suited to a relationship with a Virgin or Latent Angel. Clearly there are advantages and disadvantages to entering into a relationship with each of the Angel types, and these are outlined in the chapters for each individual Angel in Part II.

You need to recognise the advantages and disadvantages and aim to develop a relationship with the most appropriate type of Angel for you. In other words, this analysis suggests that you must think very clearly about the kind of financial and non-financial support you require from a Business Angel, and seek to choose your Angel accordingly.

Our research also highlights a series of general factors entrepreneurs need to take into account when looking for Angel investors. Foremost among these is the issue of venture location. Currently entrepreneurs are advised to confine themselves to seeking local Angel investors. This policy prescription reflects the existing research base, which strongly maintains that Angels are interested in financing only local ventures. However, we have found that most angels do not feel restricted by location, and so you should not necessarily confine yourself to looking for a local Business Angel. The survey also revealed that Angels consider trust/faith in the entrepreneur, and personal industry sector experience to be the most important factors in their investment decision. This suggests that you should start by trying to find Angels with backgrounds in your own industry, and also concentrate more on developing a personal relationship with a potential Angel once you have identified them.

The most important criterion Angels use when deciding whether or not to invest in new or early stage business is their impression of the founder and/or management team. Although we found that Angels have a variety of different preferences in terms of the form and type of proposal they receive from entrepreneurs. More specifically, we found that some Angels like to hold immediate meetings with entrepreneurs, some prefer a comprehensive business plan, while others prefer to obtain the kind of summaries currently offered by business introduction services. In general, Virgin and Latent Angels place a greater emphasis on the business plan, while the other Angel types are more concerned with holding face-to-face meetings with the entrepreneur.

IMPROVING THE EFFICIENCY OF THE INFORMAL VENTURE CAPITAL MARKET

Business introduction services aim to marry up entrepreneurs with investors. In Chapter 14 we outline how the process works and provide profiles of business introduction services operating in the UK.

We feel that the business introduction services in operation today are too passive. In many cases they are more publishing houses than marriage bureaux. As a result business introduction services do not represent an important source of investment proposals for Business Angels. Indeed, only 13 per cent of the 467 deals we analysed resulted from the involvement of business introduction services. Friends/family (35 per cent) and business contacts (23 per cent) were found to be much more important sources. This is a surprisingly low figure considering that the Angels who participated in this study were all either current, former or potential subscribers to one of a selected group of business introduction services. It is important to understand, however, that both active Angels and inactive Angels consider the personality of the venture founder to be the single most important investment criterion when assessing investment proposals. It is likely that Angels can be more certain of an entrepreneur's character if they are acquainted before being approached for funding. It is probably difficult for Angels to satisfactorily determine this character issue solely from a case study and a small number of subsequent meetings. For this reason we feel that business introduction services need to take on a more active role in the matchmaking process. In many cases this will involve more than simply featuring an entrepreneur in some form of monthly publication and will require them to use more interactive mechanisms such as seminars, presentations, databases, tele-matching, etc.

With regard to the style and content of the specific profiles that are featured in the publications of business introduction services, we found that Angels have a variety of preferences: 44 per cent prefer to receive proposals written by the entrepreneurs themselves, and 35 per cent prefer to have the proposals written up by the staff of the business introduction services. The number who prefer the entrepreneur's version feel that they get a greater insight into the quality of the founder/management team of the venture, while those preferring the objective business introduction service version benefit from the vetting of the staff at those organisations. Perhaps business introduction services need to cater to both of these markets.

We are also interested in examining the attitudes of Business Angels to the structure, organisation, and operation of business introduction services. Most of the current research in this area (in the UK, Mason and Harrison, 1991; in the USA, Wetzel and Freear, 1993) has argued that business introduction services should be run either on a not-for-profit basis or by the government. Our own research found that almost twice as many Angels would prefer to see these organisations run on a for-profit basis than on a not-for-profit basis, while only 5 per cent wanted them to be government operated. A summary of our findings is given in Table 2.1.

Most of the current business introduction services are operated on a regional basis. This in part reflects the belief of many researchers in both Britain and the USA that Angels prefer to invest locally. We found that Business Angels are looking for the best investment opportunities and do not generally restrict themselves to making investments in locally based ventures. We also sought the views of Angels on whether they would like to see a national network linking selected business introduction services. Almost two-thirds of

Table 2.1 Summary Findings on the Organisation and Operation of Business
Introduction Services (BISs)

Views of Angels	Past research findings	Our findings
Importance of BISs as source for current investments	Low	Low
Organisation type that best operates BISs	Not for profit	For profit
Preferred geographic scope of BISs	Regional	National
Should BISs provide corporate financing advice to Angels?	No	Yes

them supported the concept of a nationally focused business introduction service. This finding supports the conclusion of a 1993 study by the National Westminster Bank, which argues for the creation of a nationwide referral system, but seriously challenges the work of Mason and Harrison (1993) which supports regional business introduction services. More importantly this research questions the current policy of the Department of Trade and Industry, which sponsors a number of regionally focused private investor networks.

Our research has found that many inexperienced Angels would be more willing to make informal investments if they could receive advice on making and structuring them. A large number of the active Angels in this study would like to see business introduction services broaden their range of services to include the option of a corporate financing advisory role. The provision of this service would be particularly attractive to Virgin and Latent Angels—nearly three-quarters of these Angels indicated they would like to see business introduction services provide this kind of advice. In this regard, our research supports the views of an American study conducted by Freear, Sohl and Wetzel in 1994, which argued that inactive Angels need specific technical assistance to encourage them to make informal investments.

3
A Typical Informal Investment Deal

One of the distinctive features of our work has been the ability to find the fundamental characteristics of a typical informal investment deal. Our conclusions are drawn from an examination of almost 500 separate deals involving more than 200 different Business Angels. Such a scale of research has not previously been attempted and the findings of it have important implications both for entrepreneurs looking to structure an equity finance deal and Business Angels seeking to make profitable equity investments in new and growing businesses. This chapter looks at the result of our research, first summarising the key features of investment deals and then looking at the nature of the businesses that receive Angel finance, the financial structure and performance of these deals, and the non-financial contribution that Angels bring to these deals.

A typical informal investment deal

- Average total amount invested   £113 000
- Average initial amount invested   £75 000
- Average number of rounds of investment   1.8
- Average number of co-investors   2.6
- Average size of equity stake taken   35%
- Average annual rate of return   58%

On average, Business Angels invest £113 000 per deal in slightly fewer than two separate rounds of investment. Approximately two-thirds of the funds are invested in the initial round. This corresponds to a far higher level of investment than has been suggested by previous British researchers (see

Atkin and Esiri, 1993; KPMG, 1992; Mason and Harrison and associates, 1991–95). Informal investment appears to have been surprisingly profitable for Angels—the average annual rate of return earned was 58 per cent[1]. This level of return suggests that, where a business survives the start-up phase, both entrepreneurs and Angels can make considerable returns on their initial investment. Typically these deals do not involve large numbers of investors: an average of 2.6 additional investors (including the entrepreneur/venture manager) participated with the Business Angel in each deal. However, entrepreneurs do need to be aware that they are likely to be dealing with more than one investor. This has advantages in terms of the enhanced range of experiences multiple investors can bring to a venture, but obviously impacts in a negative way on the share of equity entrepreneurs may be required to pass on to investors. Only a third of Business Angels were found to have an explicit preference for majority stakeholdings and the average size of stakeholding was found to be 35 per cent. This suggests that Angels like to take substantial, but still minority, stakes in the ventures they finance.

THE NATURE OF BUSINESS VENTURES THAT RECEIVE ANGEL FINANCE

Our research sought to determine the size of the ventures that received Angel finance, their stage of development and the manner in which the investors became aware of the deals. Our findings are summarised in Figure 3.1. The majority (55 per cent) of the deals we examined involved start-up finance, but significant subsets existed involving expansion finance (25 per cent) and finance for management buy-outs or buy-ins (10 per cent). It appears that Business Angels are indeed attempting to fill the finance gap that many British and American researchers (CBI, 1993; Mason and Harrison, 1991) believe exists for the supply of seed, start-up and early stage capital to entrepreneurs. In fact, by providing this early stage capital, Business Angels are complementing, rather than competing with, the formal venture capital industry that now concentrates on providing development capital and funds for management buy-outs or buy-ins (see BVCA, 1992; Murray, 1994).

The initial size and growth of the ventures that receive Angel finance is also of considerable interest. Turnover (sales) and employee number were deemed the most appropriate measures to indicate the size and growth of these ventures. To put values on these measures, we asked Business Angels to detail the initial and current turnover and employee number for each of the ventures in which they had invested during the preceding three-year period.

Our research suggests that the business ventures that receive informal venture capital have very high growth potential (more than 200 per cent in under three years). It is particularly interesting to compare these levels of actual

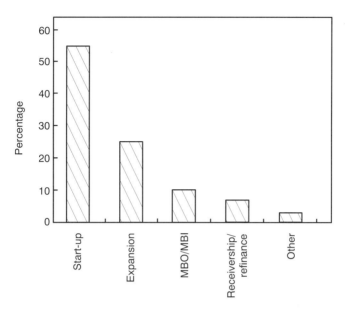

Figure 3.1 Development Stage of the Ventures in which Angels Invest

growth for the businesses that Angels finance with the growth expectations they have prior to making their investments. The average minimum rate Business Angels expect their investment to grow at is 22 per cent per annum (a compounded three year figure of 82 per cent). This figure is very similar to the desired minimum annual growth level of 20 per cent highlighted by Wetzel and Freear (1993) in America.

Whether you use sales turnover or employee number as a proxy for growth, it is clear that the actual level of growth achieved tends dramatically to exceed the minimum growth expectations Angels may have. These growth levels are exceptionally high given that they have been achieved in less than three years, and they point to the economic importance of Angels in providing start-up and early stage finance to these high growth ventures. From an entrepreneur's point of view, these findings suggest that the equity finance packages offered by Business Angels represent a very suitable form of finance for potential high growth ventures.

In a 1992 report on businesses in the UK, Stanworth, Purdy and Kirby identified a "growth corridor" for new and growing businesses. They found that only 20 per cent of new businesses enter this growth corridor by employing more than five people, and that only 2 per cent emerge from it by subsequently expanding to employ more than 50 people. This research suggests that most of the ventures Angels finance are in this growth corridor, and that a large number of the ventures are progressing quickly through it.

The Size and Growth of Ventures Receiving Informal Finance

- Average initial turnover (sales) of the ventures   £908 000
- Average current turnover (sales) of the ventures   £2 110 000
- Average growth in turnover (sales)   230%
- Average initial number of employees   16
- Average current number of employees   34
- Average growth in employee number   210%

We also sought to discover the manner by which Angels came into contact with these deals. Our research found that friends/family (35 per cent) and business associates (23 per cent) are the most common sources. The fact that these two groups account for 58 per cent of all deals, reinforces the findings of some existing British research (National Westminster Bank, 1993), which found that personal contact and business acquaintances were the principal information source for Angels, and that business introduction services played a minor role.

THE FINANCIAL STRUCTURE AND PERFORMANCE OF ANGEL DEALS

The overall level of finance Business Angels bring to new and growing businesses and the timing of that finance is of particular interest to entrepreneurs considering using this form of funding to develop their ventures. We specifically examined the level of initial investment, along with the number and size of subsequent investment rounds provided by Business Angels. This section also focuses on the incidence of co-investment and syndication, the size of equity stakes taken by Angels, and the expected and realised rates of return they earn from the ventures.

We found that the mean figure for average total investment per Angel per venture was approximately £113 000. Such a level of total investment per deal is significantly larger than the figure of £10 000 suggested by previous British researchers (Mason and Harrison, 1994a; an earlier study by Mason, Harrison and Chaloner, 1991a, found that LINC (Local Investment Network Company) investors typically invested less than £50 000 in each deal).

That there is such a contrast between these figures is particularly important, because versions of this figure quoted by previous British researchers have had meaningful policy implications. The Department of Trade and Industry has established a range of small, locally based institutes using the Training and Enterprise Councils (TECs) to promote informal investment. The premise behind the decision to use small-scale, locally focused institutes to promote informal investment has been the belief that Angels make infrequent (one or two investments every three years), low-level (about £20 000) investments in locally based ventures.

This study has found a whole group of Business Angels with a very different pattern of investment activity. These investors make more than two investments every three years and invest an average of £113 000 per venture. We also found that the perception that Angels feel restricted to investing in their own locality is inaccurate. In short, this study suggests that the "pillars of thought" behind the current government policies for the promotion of informal investment may need to be re-examined.

Levels of Angel Investment per Deal	
• Average size of initial investment	£75 000
• Average number of deals having more than one round of investment	55%
• Average size of subsequent investment	£70 000
• Average size of overall investment	£113 000

While we were interested in examining the total amount Business Angels invest in new and growing businesses, the breakdown of these financial packages is also of interest. It is clear that the mean levels of initial investment (about £75 000) found in this survey are substantially higher than those reported by previous researchers in this field. In fact, the initial level of investment tends to account for about two-thirds of the total investment. However, in 55 per cent of the deals we examined the Angels provided more than one round of finance. This is substantially higher than the findings of a 1995 study by Mason, Harrison and Allen, who reported that staged funding was provided in only 21 per cent of the deals they examined. They did suggest, however, that staged funding may be more common for total investments of over £50 000. We found that where subsequent rounds of investment were made the average amount provided was £70 000.

It is clear from this analysis that Angels do not just provide initial, start-up finance but also continue to provide the ventures with the capital as they progress from the start-up stage, although the number of rounds of financing tends to remain fairly low. In only 7 per cent of the deals were three or more financing rounds provided. On average the mean number of subsequent rounds of investment was found to be 0.8. Nevertheless, the incidence of subsequent Angel investment does suggest that many Angels have an ongoing financing relationship with the ventures they support.

Most British researchers have argued that Business Angels co-invest relatively infrequently with other Angels and/or institutions. For instance, Mason,
Harrison and Allen (1995) and Mason and Harrison (1993) found that only
about a third of all informal direct investments were syndicated. This con-
trasts sharply with two studies published in the USA in 1989—one by Arum
and the other by Gaston—which both found that about 92 per cent of the
deals they examined involved some level of co-investment. Arun found that
an average of 4.4 Angels participated in each venture investment. We sought
to determine whether or not such a large difference between the US and
British experiences really exists and were concerned both with investigating
the overall incidence of co-investment activity and with identifying the number of co-investors participating in each deal.

We found that in the majority of cases Angels had one or more co-investors
(including the venture founder/manager) involved with them in financing a
venture; only 27 per cent of the deals involved no co-investment (see Figure
3.2). More than half of the deals (52 per cent) involved Angels entering into a
deal with two or more other investors. An average of 2.6 co-investors (or 3.6
investors in total) were involved in each deal. The incidence of co-investment
in the deals examined in this study tends to mirror but understate the American case as highlighted by Arum in his 1989 study. For instance, he found that
Angels had co-invested in 92 per cent of the cases versus an incidence of 73
per cent found in this research. He also found an average of 4.4 investors per
deal versus the 3.6 identified by this project. While the level of co-investment

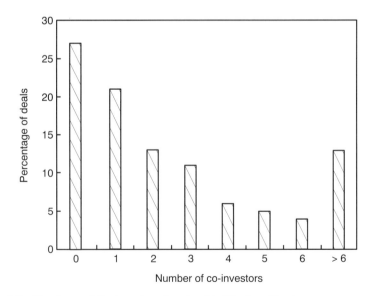

Figure 3.2   Numbers of Co-investors Involved in Venture Deals

among the Business Angels in this study falls slightly below the American case, it is certainly higher than suggested by previous British research groups.

We also wanted to find out whether there was an increase in the level of co-investment as the ventures grew in size, and if their capital requirements increased. Our work suggests that the incidence of co-investment increases slightly as the ventures grow in size. For example, in 27 per cent of the ventures the Angel had no co-investors at the outset, but this number falls to 19 per cent when the current position of the ventures is reported. Such an increase in the number of Angel investors is entirely expected because as businesses grow and their financing needs increase, it is likely that new investors will be required to meet these needs. In some cases the existing investors will provide extra funding, but where ventures are unable to draw extra funds from these original Angels they will often appeal to other informal sources to meet their capital requirements.

The typical size of the equity stake Business Angels take in these ventures is also of great interest to both entrepreneurs seeking finance and to Angels looking to provide it. We found that the mean size initially taken by the Angel investor was 35 per cent. This represents a sizeable shareholding and gives the Business Angel a considerable influence in the decision-making of the venture. More than a third of the respondents to the survey had an explicit preference for majority shareholdings, while a roughly similar number were solely interested in minority stakes. An average shareholding of 35 per cent represents a midpoint between the two. This supports the findings of the 1995 study by Mason, Harrison and Allen, which found that 56 per cent of Angels take minority shareholdings in the ventures they finance. It is interesting to note that we also found that there was little meaningful difference between the initial and current stakeholdings of the Angel investors. This may appear surprising given that the number of co-investors involved in the ventures tends to increase with time. However, it is possible that it is the venture founders or managers, and not the original Business Angels, who are obliged to give up some of their shareholding when new investors are introduced.

While most of the Angel investors were found to take minority shareholdings, it is clear that they still take sizeable stakes (average 35 per cent) in the ventures they back. The findings from this research suggests that informal investors tend to take larger equity stakes than formal venture capital companies. For example, the 1995 edition of the *Venture Capital Report Guide to Venture Capital in the UK and Europe* (Cary, 1995) found that most British venture capital companies take stakes of between 10 per cent and 30 per cent in the ventures they support, and that on average they take stakes of less than 25 per cent. Clearly venture capital firms come in at a later stage in the investment process than Business Angels, and as a result invest considerably larger amounts of money. However, they do not appear to have the same degree of control, in terms of equity, as Business Angel investors.

An examination of the actual deals in which Business Angels provide finance to new and growing ventures suggests that this form of investment is extremely profitable. No previous study has been able to determine the actual rate of return earned by Business Angels on their investments. The average annual rate of return earned on each of the actual deals was 58 per cent per annum. This figure is surprisingly high and is more than double the expected rate of return of 27 per cent. This level of return points to the highly profitable nature of informal investment. The differential between the actual and expected rates of return mirrors the difference between the actual and expected rates of growth that was explained earlier. Most Business Angels are attracted to make informal investments by the opportunity to earn higher financial returns than those offered by quoted shares. An annual return of 58 per cent clearly represents such an opportunity. Therefore it comes as no surprise that in 77 per cent of the deals the participating Angels expressed satisfaction with how the deal had worked out.

It is interesting to compare the rate of return the Angels expected to earn on the specific deals in which they actually participated, with the more general minimum expected rates of return cited by all of the Business Angels who responded to the survey. The mean minimum expected rate of return for all the active Angels in the sample was found to be only 19 per cent. However, when these Angels examined specific deal proposals, to which they ultimately provided finance, their expected rate of return rose to 27 per cent. This represents an increased expectation of almost 50 per cent and suggests that there are many opportunities available to Business Angels that exceed their minimum financial expectations.

In a 1987 study Robinson found that most American venture capital companies demand and earn annualised rates of return of between 25 per cent and 40 per cent on their investments. We found that informal investors tend to accept projects with slightly lower expected returns than the formal venture capital sector. This almost certainly reflects the contention made by many researchers (Baty, 1991; Sullivan and Miller, 1990; Wetzel, 1983, 1987) that informal investors are willing to trade some financial returns for non-financial benefits. We have also found that, despite the fact that Business Angels accept lower expected returns than venture capital companies, the actual rates of return they earn on their investments may be even higher than the actual returns earned by formal venture capital companies.

The investments Business Angels make in new and growing ventures tend to be medium or long-term investments in that they take a longer-term view than other suppliers of risk capital. For example, in a 1983 article Wetzel argues that venture capital companies tend to expect the start-up businesses they support to be able to go public in less than five years so that they can recoup their investment. On the other hand, he suggests that ventures supported by Business Angels are unlikely to go public in less than five years.

Mason and Harrison (1993) distinguish British Angels from their American counterparts by suggesting that they have a lower exit horizon of three to five years. We found that Business Angels plan to exit the businesses they finance after an average of six years.

THE POST-INVESTMENT ACTIVITY OF BUSINESS ANGELS

One of the distinguishing features of Business Angel investors is the "value-added" component they tend to bring to their investee companies. We were interested in clarifying the exact nature of this value-added component, and in particular sought to examine the role that Business Angels play in the businesses after they have provided the finance. Our findings are illustrated in Figure 3.3.

In 48 per cent of the ventures the Angels indicated that their experience/ expertise was the principal non-financial resource they brought to the ventures. Wetzel and Freear (1993) point out that the value-added benefit an Angel's non-financial contribution brings to the venture is an enormous hidden benefit to the entrepreneur. For almost half of the ventures analysed, the expertise and experience of the Business Angels in the operation and financing of small businesses constitutes the principal value-added benefit.

It was very interesting to find that in more than a third (34 per cent) of the deals, Angels pointed to a formal management role and/or a full-time job as representing their greatest non-financial contribution. In these instances Angel investors are becoming actively involved on a day-to-day basis in the

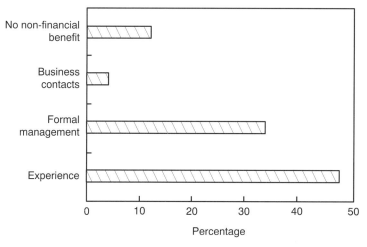

Figure 3.3 Non-financial Benefits Angels feel they bring to Investee Businesses

operation of the ventures they have financed. Such a level of commitment clearly extends beyond being a mere "sounding board" for the entrepreneur, to taking on an active role in the management of the venture. This desire of a substantial minority of Angels to take on a full-time role in the ventures they finance mirrors the more general investment motives of Angels. A third of the active Angels whom we examined cited the desire to create a job/income for themselves as the principal reason for attracting them to make informal investments.

Quite clearly, Angels investing for these reasons represent an important subset of the overall population of Angels surveyed. At a more general level, it is very clear that the vast majority of Angels feel that they can bring more than just finance to the ventures they support. In only 12 per cent of the cases did Angels feel that they brought no non-financial benefit to their investments.

Given that Business Angels offer such a value-added component to the ventures they finance, and more particularly offer assistance to the founders and managers of those ventures, we were interested in examining the nature of the post-investment relationship between the Angel and the venture founder. Our research found that in 83 per cent of the cases the relationship the Angels had with their entrepreneurs was positive, and that a negative relationship existed in only 11 per cent of the cases.

Our research reveals that in 82 per cent of the cases Angels either take on a formal management role, or they offer the benefits of their experience/ expertise to the venture founder. Clearly both of these roles require a level of contact between the Angel and the venture. We were interested in clarifying the exact nature of the contact between the Angel and the full-time management of the venture. In an attempt to estimate the level of contact, the annual number of visits and phone calls made to the venture were used as proxies for the level of contact. The research found that the average number of visits Angels made to their investments each year was 58—more than one visit a week. This research also found that Business Angels make an average of 83 phone calls per year to each of their ventures. While the length and purpose of each visit and phone call could not be determined, the high level of contact suggests that Angels play an active role in the operation and management of their investments.

These findings build on the results of the study of Mason, Harrison and Allen in 1995, which found that about half of the Angels they profiled visited their ventures about once a week. The level of contact found by this study may also be slightly higher than that of many formal venture capital companies. For example, in 1987 Robinson estimated that venture capital companies spend an average of 31 days a year providing managerial assistance to the ventures they finance. However, Harrison and Mason (1992) contend that the main difference in the post-investment roles of informal and formal investors is qualitative, in terms of type and purpose, rather than quantitative. For example, they argue that, compared to the venture capitalist, the informal investor is seeking to manage and monitor the "venture", not the "investment".

NOTE

1. An annual rate of return of 58 per cent seems surprisingly high. One possible explanation is that Angels report only on ventures that have been profitable. No data on the losses incurred when investee businesses collapsed was available.

PART II
Identifying Your Perfect Angel

4
The Entrepreneur Angel

Entrepreneur Angels are the most active and experienced informal investors and as a result represent a particularly appealing source of finance for the first-time entrepreneur. These investors are individuals who make frequent, large-scale investments in new and growing ventures. Entrepreneur Angels are considerably wealthier than other individual Angel types and have been more entrepreneurial in their own business careers. While they invest principally for financial gain, these Angels are also attracted by the fun and satisfaction of making informal investments. This chapter focuses on the investment activity, the personal and business characteristics, the investment preferences and expectations, and the non-financial contribution of these Entrepreneur Angels.

INVESTMENT ACTIVITY OF ENTREPRENEUR ANGELS

Entrepreneur Angels are more active investors than the other individual Angel types, both in terms of the total level of funds they invest and the number of separate ventures they back. Almost half of Entrepreneur Angels have invested more than £500 000 in unquoted ventures over the past three years, while the average amount invested was £590 000, according to our research. This figure is considerably higher than the figures of £131 000 and £35 000 for Wealth Maximising Angels and Income Seeking Angels respectively. Our experience is that Entrepreneur Angels are primarily interested in larger opportunities and are not limited to just one or two investments.

Entrepreneur Angels typically back a higher number of ventures than other types of Angels, and they are often more open to considering additional opportunities.

On average, we found Entrepreneur Angels invest £174 000 per deal, in two separate rounds of investment, with approximately two-thirds of the funds

---

Overall Investment Activity of Entrepreneur Angels

- Average number of investments   3.4
- Total amount invested   £590 000
- Percentage investing more than £500 000   43%

---

being invested in the initial round. This size of deal is slightly lower than the typical Corporate Angel deal, but notably larger than those for Wealth Maximising and Income Seeking Angels. Entrepreneur Angels also take large stakes in the ventures they back. Almost half of these Angels have a preference for a majority stake, while the average size of their stakeholding is almost 40 per cent. Typically these deals do not involve large numbers of co-investors. However, an average of 2.3 additional investors (including the founder/venture manager) participated with the Entrepreneur Angel in each deal. These deals are extremely profitable—in fact, Entrepreneur Angels earn significantly higher returns on their deals than the other Angel types.

A Typical Entrepreneur Angel Deal

- Average total amount invested   £174 000
- Average initial amount invested   £111 000
- Average number of rounds of investment   2.0
- Average number of co-investors   2.3
- Average size of equity stake taken   38%
- Average annual rate of return   61%

Almost two-thirds of the investments made by Entrepreneur Angels were made at the start-up stage. Generally they prefer to "get in" on the bottom floor of a budding business; they don't want to be part of a firm that is well on the road to maturity. This represents a slightly higher level of start-up investment than that for the other Angel types.

CHARACTERISTICS OF ENTREPRENEUR ANGELS

The fundamental traits of Business Angels are very similar across the different types of Angels. Entrepreneur Angels share these common traits in that they are almost exclusively:

- male
- middle-aged (average age 52 years)
- well educated (32 per cent have university degrees and 43 per cent have technical/professional training).

However, Entrepreneur Angels do tend to be older, richer and more entrepreneurial than other individual (i.e. not corporate) Angel types. Though these demographics are helpful in identifying Angels, it is more important to seek to understand the mindset and then find individuals that match the profile, regardless of gender, age or education.

The most important differences between the Entrepreneur Angels and other Angel types are their financial and business backgrounds. Entrepreneur Angels are extremely wealthy: almost three-quarters of this group were worth more than £1 million (even after excluding their principal residence), and the majority continue to earn in excess of £100 000 a year. As with all Business Angels, these investors tend to be almost entirely self-made. More Entrepreneur Angels derive their wealth from their own business(es) than was the case for Wealth Maximising Angels or Income Seeking Angels. Indeed, less than ten per cent of Entrepreneur Angels in our research listed inheritance as their principal source of wealth. This financial background sets Entrepreneur Angels apart from Wealth Maximising and Income Seeking Angels, which have lower net worth and annual incomes. These Angels are more likely to be impressed by achievement in the "real world" than academic credentials or family background. In order to gain their attention we suggest that you first seek to establish a rapport and then quickly move on to a hard-nosed review of your business plan.

We found considerable differences in the entrepreneurial backgrounds of Angel types. On average, Entrepreneurial Angels start four substantial new businesses (businesses with more than five staff and/or a turnover of more than £1 million) during the course of their own business careers. This rate of entrepreneurship represents a key difference between this group and Wealth Maximising and Income Seeking Angels, which had founded 1.3 and 0.4 new businesses respectively. It is clear that these Angels have considerable first-hand experience in establishing and growing new businesses. To many entrepreneurs, access to this range of experiences can be as useful as access to the financial resources of Entrepreneur Angels.

INVESTMENT CRITERIA AND EXPECTATIONS OF ENTREPRENEUR ANGELS

To win these investors over to your investment it is helpful to understand the reasons why they invest and what they expect to get from it. We found that Entrepreneur Angels invest in unquoted ventures for fun and satisfaction as well as for financial returns, and that they consider the personality of the venture founder to be the most important criterion when deciding who to invest with. Baty (1991) found that Business Angels are sufficiently wealthy not to actually need the returns from a successful investment—they choose to invest for personal satisfaction and the excitement of the process. With this in mind, it is interesting to note that for over 85 per cent of their deals, Entrepreneur Angels in our study had enjoyed making investments in start-ups, the highest level of satisfaction among all the Angel types.

Over half the Entrepreneur Angels we spoke to highlighted personality of the founder/manager of the venture as being their most important investment criterion. Almost a third of Entrepreneur Angels believe that their current investment activity is restricted by a lack of faith in the prospective founders/ managers who approach them for funding. In our experience Entrepreneur Angels will relatively quickly decide whether they feel comfortable with the founder/manager of an opportunity they are investigating—we suggest that neither side invest too much time if the chemistry is negative from the start. Entrepreneur Angels do appear to be successful in appraising their prospective managers: for 90 per cent of the ventures we looked at, they indicated that they were satisfied with their relationship with the management.

Their own experience in the industry sector is the most important investment criterion for only one-fifth of Entrepreneur Angels. Of all the Angel types, they are the most open to investing in ventures outside their own field of experience, so don't be afraid of proposing a new type of venture to them. Each of the other Angel types placed a greater importance on experience in the particular industry sector when allocating their funds. This may well reflect the fact that the other Angel types intend to play a more active day-to-day role in the running of their ventures.

In general, Entrepreneur Angels do not consider venture location to be an important investment criterion: less than 5 per cent cite this as their most important criterion. Almost half would be willing to invest more than 200 miles from their place of work, while only 3 per cent feel restricted to investing within 50 miles of their workplace. This is contrary to the popular view that Business Angels will only invest close to home.

Entrepreneur Angel Expectations of Deals

- Level of co-investment   52% like co-investment
- Size of shareholding   41% prefer majority stakes
- Venture size (turnover)   £2 000 000 (5-year)
- Expected rate of annual return   22%
- Timeframe for exit   6 years

An encouraging piece of news for entrepreneurs is that almost two-thirds of Entrepreneur Angels hope that their investment activity will increase in the next five years. Given this aspiration, it is important to look at the reasons that have restricted their investment activity to date, and to examine the factors they feel would encourage them to increase their rate of investment.

All Angel types cite a lack of suitable proposals as the single biggest factor restricting their investment activity. The principal information sources for Entrepreneur Angels are friends/family (37 per cent) and business associates (25 per cent).

While all Angel types point to the lack of quality business proposals as restricting their investment activity, large differences emerge in the relative importance of some of the other factors. Roughly a third of Entrepreneur Angels point to problems with the founder/manager and the reliability of their information as restricting their investment activity. It is perhaps more surprising that almost a third of Entrepreneur Angels cite a lack of available funds as being a restriction. This was not found to be as important a factor for Wealth Maximising Angels (17 per cent), Income Seeking Angels (27 per cent) or Corporate Angels (18 per cent), despite the fact that the first two of these groups have smaller investment portfolios. In fact, almost two-thirds of Entrepreneur Angels have more than £100 000 available for further informal investment, and more than half have more than £500 000 available.

The top four reasons given by Entrepreneur Angels to explain why their investment activity is restricted are:

1. lack of suitable business proposals
2. lack of faith in the founder/manager
3. lack of reliable information
4. lack of experience in pricing equity stakes.

The factors that would encourage Entrepreneur Angels to increase their investment activity are given in Figure 4.1.

NON-FINANCIAL CONTRIBUTIONS OF ENTREPRENEUR ANGELS

Entrepreneur Angels are especially attractive to the novice entrepreneur. In the vast majority of cases, these Angels feel that they provide more than just capital to the ventures they finance (see Figure 4.2). Unsurprisingly, given the business backgrounds of Angels generally, each of the groups cite the experience/expertise they bring to a venture as being their principal non-financial contribution. In the case of Entrepreneur Angels, over 60 per cent feel that this experience or expertise is the most important non-financial

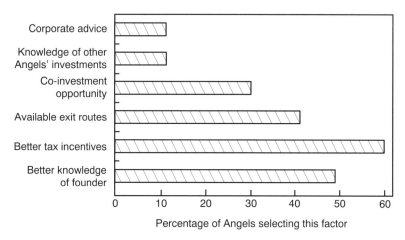

Figure 4.1 Factors that would Encourage Entrepreneur Angels to Increase their Investment Activity

benefit they bring to a venture. Almost a quarter feel that a formal management role is their most important contribution. Entrepreneur Angels differ from the other Angel types in this regard because a significantly greater number of Wealth Maximising, Income Seeking and Corporate Angels indicate that a formal management role, or even full-time employment, is their greatest non-financial contribution. This suggests that Entrepreneur Angels play a less active day-to-day role in the management of their informal investments than the other types.

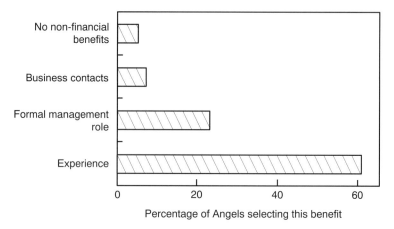

Figure 4.2 Non-financial Benefits Entrepreneur Angels feel they bring to Ventures

We also looked at the level of contact between the different Angels types and the ventures they support. In particular we were interested in the number of visits and telephone calls the Angels made to the ventures. On average, Entrepreneur Angels visit the ventures they finance about once a week and telephone them on 68 occasions during a year. We believe that these figures indicate a regular involvement in the management of their investments, and further support the idea that Angels bring substantially more than just capital to entrepreneurial ventures.

For a new entrepreneur without a great deal of experience in a particular industry or in start-ups in general Angels can potentially provide a valuable source of advice. Given the typical backgrounds of Entrepreneur Angels, a wise entrepreneur will use their Angel and consult with them on major decisions: how effectively to run the business, negotiations, marketing, and other key business tasks. Used judiciously, Entrepreneur Angels can provide an excellent source of inexpensive but first-class management consulting.

SUMMARY FOR ENTREPRENEUR ANGELS

Entrepreneur Angels are the most active and experienced informal investors and as a result represent a particularly appealing source of finance for the first-time entrepreneur. The key points to remember about Entrepreneur Angels are:

- They are individuals who make frequent, large-scale investments in new and growing ventures—they are active and ready to go ahead if you can convince them of the potential of your venture.
- They are considerably wealthier than other individual Angel types.
- They have been more entrepreneurial in their own business careers.
- Though they invest principally for financial gain, these Angels are also attracted by the fun and satisfaction of making informal investments and often interact a great deal with the founders/managers of their investments, and as such they are an excellent source of inexpensive management consulting advice.

Entrepreneurial Angel Example

LES LAURENT*

Age: 60; Location: London

Overlooking the River Thames, Les Laurent's impressive office is perched high up in one of London's more splendid Victorian buildings. It is from here that Les spends most of his time investing in various companies, including unquoted entrepreneurial start-ups. Having amassed a substantial sum from the sale of his own company, he continues to apply his business skills to the five unquoted investments and other diverse securities he has financed. With potential financial returns as more of a secondary concern, Les's main investment motivation is to be involved in the entrepreneurial process. But being part of the firm-building process is not new to him or his family.

Les was born into an entrepreneurial environment. His father successfully built up a company importing pharmaceuticals and wanted his son to follow in his footsteps. After reading history at Oxford University and gaining some experience in an oil refinery in the United States, Les joined the family firm. There he started a new division specialising in oil refining and was soon the head of new development, and later the head of business development. After proving himself in the business, he became managing director and subsequently chairman of the firm. This family business proved to be very profitable. It was sold in 1995.

With the proceeds of this sale Les established the small investment firm he now runs with his own funds.

When considering unquoted investment opportunities, Les's main complaint is that too often the business plans he sees are not believable: "If the financials are not realistic and the entrepreneurs are not convincing in their story and implementation plans, then I won't consider it further." For him, the financials are "the boring bit, but they are the essential backbone of a good business". He requires unquoted companies to formulate realistic budget projections so that if there is a subsequent deviation "we have to ask why". Another deterrent is when an entrepreneur requests an unrealistic sum of money: "If the entrepreneur does not ask for enough, and clearly needs more, then I wonder whether he has really thought through the business thoroughly." Conversely, if an "entrepreneur asks for too much money and offers too little equity and managerial control for it, I usually won't consider it further."

---

* A pseudonym was used to protect the anonymity of this Business Angel. All other data is factual and has been taken from a 90-minute interview Mark van Osnabrugge held with the Business Angel on 13 February 1996.

Like most Business Angels, Les believes that the expertise of the entrepreneurs is a very important consideration in making unquoted investments; he usually prefers to have more than one entrepreneur running the business since "two brains are better than one". Further investment considerations include the presence of a growing market, a good product with a commercial advantage, and an industry he understands well (Les prefers industrial investments). Surprisingly, Les is not too concerned with the specifics of the business or product he is funding, as long as it is commercially viable and strong.

In his latest investment in a plastics firm, Les has taken on a more passive role—monitoring the financials from afar and rendering advice only when really needed. With many other unquoted and quoted personal investments to oversee, Les is an active Business Angel who clearly is enjoying the many challenges and rewards of being part of the entrepreneurial process.

5
The Corporate Angel

Corporate Angels are companies that make Angel-type investments. They have corporate resources at their disposal and invest greater levels of funds than most individual Angel investors. Our research found that this group of Angels invest predominantly for financial gain, although a significant number choose to support unquoted ventures out of "a sense of social responsibility". This chapter looks at the investment activity, the investment preferences and expectations, and the non-financial contribution of Corporate Angels.

INVESTMENT ACTIVITY OF CORPORATE ANGELS

Corporate Angels make frequent investments in unquoted ventures and invest high levels of funds. Almost 40 per cent of this group has invested more than £500 000 in new and growing businesses and on average these Angels support about three ventures each. The average overall level of investment of Corporate Angels in informal ventures is £540 000. The overall investment activity of this group is similar to that of the Entrepreneur Angel group, who invest an average amount of £590 000 in 3.4 ventures. However, Corporate Angels tend to make larger but less frequent investments than Entrepreneur Angels. In fact, a typical Corporate Angel investment is 23 per cent larger than those made by Entrepreneur Angels. Clearly Corporate Angels have a very different pattern of investment activity to those of Wealth Maximising or Income Seeking Angels.

Corporate Angels are able to sustain this higher level of investment activity because they have significantly greater levels of funds at their disposal than the individual Angel types. For example, more than a third of Corporate Angels have more than £1 million available for investing, while only a quarter of Entrepreneur Angels, 17 per cent of Wealth Maximising Angels, and no Income Seeking Angels have portfolios of this size.

> *Overall Investment Activity of Corporate Angels*
>
> - Average number of investments   3
> - Total amount invested   £540 000
> - Percentage investing more than £500 000   38%

Corporate Angels provide extremely high levels of finance, usually take majority shareholdings in their ventures, and rarely co-invest. On average this group of Angels invest £214 000 in their ventures. About three-quarters of this sum is provided at the initial stage of investment. This size of investment is considerably higher than that provided by the private individual Angels and reflects the greater level of assets that companies generally have at their disposal. Corporate Angels also tend to take majority stakeholdings in the ventures they finance: 60 per cent of these Angels prefer majority holdings, and the average shareholding is 51 per cent. This represents a significantly greater preference for majority stakes and a considerably higher average shareholding than for the other Angel types.

> *A Typical Corporate Angel Deal*
>
> - Average total amount invested   £214 000
> - Average initial amount invested   £159 000
> - Average number of rounds of investment   1.7
> - Average number of co-investors   1.3
> - Average size of equity stake taken   51%
> - Average annual rate of return   8%

Previous research (Arum, 1989; Mason and Harrison, 1993; Wetzel and Freear, 1993) has suggested that British Business Angels are less inclined to co-invest than their American counterparts. Each of the types of Business Angels identified by this research had an average of between 2.3 and 3.0 co-investors involved in their deals. This level of co-investment is higher than suggested by previous British researchers, but still below the American level. However, Corporate Angels seem less inclined to co-invest than the other Angel types: only a quarter of this group expressed a desire to have other investors involved in their deals, while the average number of co-investors participating in each deal (including the venture founder/manager) was only 1.3. There is a very clear contrast here between Corporate Angels and the other active Angel types. Most

Entrepreneur Angels (54 per cent), Wealth Maximising Angels (60 per cent), and Income Seeking Angels (55 per cent) express a desire to have co-investors involved in their deals.

INVESTMENT PREFERENCES AND EXPECTATIONS OF CORPORATE ANGELS

Corporate Angels invest in unquoted ventures predominantly for financial gain, and the most important investment criterion for these Angels is their impression of the founder/manager of the prospective venture. A greater number of Corporate Angels (59 per cent) cite expected financial returns as being their primary investment reason than do active Angels generally. Despite the fact that financial returns are more important to Corporate Angels than to the other Angel types, they appear to earn lower rates of return on their investments than private individual Angels. Consequently, it is not surprising to note that a third of Corporate Angels are not satisfied with their Angel investments. This represents a considerably higher level of dissatisfaction than for the other Angel types.

There are other factors that impact on the investment activity of this group. In particular, almost a quarter choose to make informal investments out of a sense of social responsibility. Research in the 1980s by Wetzel (1983) found "a sense of social responsibility" to be an important influence on the investment activity of US Business Angels. Our study suggests that in general British Business Angels do not make informal investments for this reason: only 5 per cent of Entrepreneur Angels, 4 per cent of Wealth Maximising Angels, and no Income Seeking Angels rate a sense of social responsibility as their most important investment reason. Corporate Angels are a clear exception.

Principal Investment Reasons for Corporate Angels

- Expected financial return   59%
- To create income   29%
- Fun and satisfaction   24%
- Sense of social responsibility   24%

The two most important investment criteria for Corporate Angels are:

- impression of founder manager—62 per cent
- own experience in sector—27 per cent.

Nearly two-thirds of Corporate Angels consider their impression of the founder/manager of a prospective venture to be the most important investment criterion. Over half of Corporate Angels believe their current level of investment activity is curtailed because they simply do not have confidence in the people who approach them for start-up capital. This focus on the importance of the founder/manager tends to mirror the preferences of the other Angel types. A substantial number, over a quarter, of Corporate Angels consider it very important that prospective ventures be located in an industry sector in which they have experience. This preference to invest in sectors where they have experience was also found to be important for Wealth Maximising Angels, and especially for Income Seeking Angels, but was relatively unimportant in the case of Entrepreneur Angels.

Corporate Angels tend to invest more closely to their principal place of work than any of the other Angel types. On average the ventures Corporate Angels back are 54 miles away from their workplace. Only 15 per cent of Corporate Angels feel restricted to solely investing within 50 miles of their workplace, while 50 per cent are willing to invest in prospective ventures located more than 200 miles away. It is clear that Corporate Angels, like private individual Angel groups, invest locally because they tend to receive more proposals from local rather than national sources. Two-thirds of the ventures backed by this group of investors are sourced either through friends, family or business associates. It is likely that the majority of these sources are locally based. Each of the Angel types feel that their current investment activity is restricted by inefficiencies in the informal venture capital market, which make it difficult for them to locate suitable business proposals. A national network that provides Angels with a range of business proposals, regardless of their location, is clearly one way of helping to alleviate these inefficiencies.

Corporate Angels have more funds available for informal investment than any of the other Angel types. The current investment activity of Corporate Angels is restricted by a number of factors, the top four of which are:

1. lack of suitable business proposals
2. lack of faith in the founder/manager
3. lack of reliable information
4. lack of available funds.

The two principal "restrictors" are a lack of suitable business proposals (77 per cent), and a lack of faith in the venture founder or manager (50 per cent). Almost three-quarters of Corporate Angels we studied stated that better access to suitable proposals during the past three years would have increased their investment activity. Corporate Angels were also found to have a greater concern with the trustworthiness of venture founders than any of the other Angel types. This concern may well reflect the constraints of making invest-

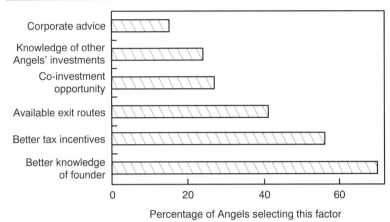

Figure 5.1 Factors that would Encourage Corporate Angels to Increase their Investment Activity

ments on behalf of a company rather than as an individual. To reach these important sources of capital an entrepreneur must aggressively seek them out.

For entrepreneurs the positive news is that almost two-thirds of Corporate Angels, in common with the other Business Angel types identified by the survey, expect that their investment activity will increase over the next five years. Our study found that Corporate Angels have considerable resources available specifically for informal investment. Nearly two-thirds of Corporate Angels have more than £200 000 available for further informal investments, and almost a quarter have more than £1 million available.

We found that most Business Angels feel that developing a better relationship with the founder/manager of a prospective venture is the most important factor in increasing their future levels of investment (see Figure 5.1). Over half of Corporate Angels also expressed a desire to see improved tax incentives; this mirrors the desire of Entrepreneur Angels, who also invest extensively in the informal capital market. It is also considerably higher than those of the Wealth Maximising and Income Seeking Angel groups which invest considerably lower levels of funds.

NON-FINANCIAL CONTRIBUTION OF CORPORATE ANGELS

We found that Corporate Angels also bring a non-financial contribution to the ventures they finance. Over half say the biggest contribution they make is to bring the experience or expertise of the company to the venture founder (see Figure 5.2). More than a third of Corporate Angels point to the formal

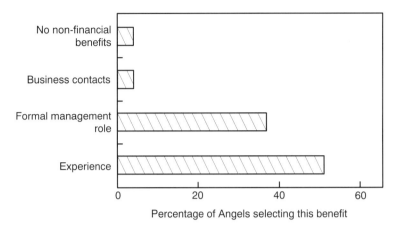

Figure 5.2   Non-financial Benefits Corporate Angels feel they bring to Ventures

role that one or more people from the company take up in the venture, as representing their biggest non-financial contribution. In this regard Corporate Angels resemble Income Seeking Angels, although it is likely that the kind of formal roles taken on are very different in each case.

Corporate Angels visit their ventures slightly less often than the other Angel types: they make an average of 45 on-site visits a year. Furthermore, they make an average of more than two telephone calls a week to the ventures, which is more than those made by the individual Angel types. It is clear that by establishing such a regular level of contact each of these Business Angels are taking on an active role in the operation of the businesses they finance.

SUMMARY FOR CORPORATE ANGELS

Corporate Angels are companies that make Angel type investments. The key points to remember about Corporate Angels are:

- They have corporate resources at their disposal and invest greater levels of funds than most individual Angel investors.
- They invest predominantly for financial gain.
- They often take an active role in the operation of the businesses they finance.
- Most Corporate Angels feel that developing a better relationship with the founder/manager of a prospective venture is the most important factor in increasing their future levels of investment.

Corporate Angel Example

JOHN GILES* (investing on behalf of family firm)

Age: 33; Location: Worcester

Wishing to diversify the family business out of its concentration in property development, John Giles has made three investments in unquoted start-up companies over the last few years. The primary motivation for these investments is financial and the amounts invested in these small firms is significantly larger than those usually invested by the other types of Business Angels. John's latest investment is in a fashion company. Although clearly there are few synergistic resources between this investment and the family's property development company, the business experience that John (who has an MBA) and his family have gained over the years has been beneficial to the start-up firm.

John's family firm is primarily involved in residential and commercial property development and investment. To get involved in unquoted small firm investments may thus seem unusual, but John lists three reasons for doing so. First, the expected financial returns on a small firm investment may render a significant long-term gain for the family business. Financial returns were rarely calculated in detail by John, but he felt that most of these risky unquoted firms had the potential to deliver the "all or nothing" chance of very high returns. Secondly, unquoted investments diversify the family firm out of its primary business concentration. Thirdly, there is the added interest of being involved in the entrepreneurial process and the fun and satisfaction that building a start-up business renders.

Like the many other types of Business Angels, Corporate Angels look for similar characteristics before deciding to fund an unquoted firm. John's primary concern was that he and his family were convinced that the "unquoted business was viable, with realistic and achievable goals". Further to this, the relationship with the entrepreneur was also paramount. The entrepreneur must have experience, talent and be able to have a good working relationship with the investors. The market is also of concern. John stated that he was particularly attracted to his latest unquoted investment in the fashion industry because it is in a niche market with good growth potential. Like other Corporate Angels, John and his family usually prefer to invest without co-investors. For them, "negotiating a deal with the other investors [in addition to the entrepreneur] is too much of a hassle".

---

* A pseudonym was used to protect the anonymity of the Business Angel. All other data is factual and has been taken from a 90-minute interview Mark van Osnabrugge held with the Business Angel on 18 April 1996.

John and his family have been semi-actively involved in their unquoted investments, rendering assistance to the firms when it is needed. With two small firm investments in their portfolio (another was recently exited), John and his family are not looking to make further unquoted investments in the near future; instead, they will concentrate on the progress of the ones they have. These are often "long-term investments in which many things have to be catered to, to make them work". With such a realistic view on the nature of his small firm investments, John is continuing to guide them to potential long-term gains.

6

The Income Seeking Angel

Income Seeking Angels are active individual investors who have made one or two low-level investments over the past three years. These Angels are well-off but not as wealthy as the other Angel types. They make their investments both for financial gain and to generate a job/income for themselves. This chapter focuses on the investment activity, personal and business characteristics, investment preferences and expectations, and the non-financial contribution that these Angels bring to the ventures they support.

INVESTMENT ACTIVITY OF INCOME SEEKING ANGELS

Income Seeking Angels have generally made one or two investments in unquoted ventures during the past three years. They have also invested less than £50 000 in total during that period. This group of Angels provide finance for an average of 1.5 investments and invest an average total of £35 000. Only 42 per cent of Income Seeking Angels make more than one investment, and only a quarter invest more than £50 000 in that period. It is clear that the investment activity of Income Seeking Angels is dramatically lower than that of the other Angel types, both in terms of the number of ventures backed and the total level of funds invested. This level of investment activity closely resembles that of Business Angels as depicted in the bulk of British management literature (e.g. Atkin and Esiri, 1993; KPMG, 1992; Mason and Harrison and associates, 1991–95).

Our research examined 71 separate deals involving 48 different Income Seeking Angels. We found that on average Income Seeking Angels invest a total of £24 000. In two-thirds of our cases these Angels provided only one round of financing. The size of these individual investment deals is significantly below those of Entrepreneur, Wealth Maximising and Corporate

> *Overall Investment Activity of Income Seeking Angels*
>
> - Average number of investments   1.5
> - Total amount invested   £35 000
> - Percentage investing more than £50 000   27%

Angels. The average number of co-investors (including the venture founder/manager) participating in these deals is 3.0, almost a third of deals involving five or more co-investors. Only slightly more than a quarter of Income Seeking Angels had a preference for taking majority stakeholdings in the ventures they financed. The average shareholding value of 20 per cent reflects this and is lower than those taken by the other Angel types.

> *A Typical Income Seeking Angel Deal*
>
> - Average total amount invested   £24 000
> - Average initial amount invested   £17 000
> - Average number of rounds of investment   1.5
> - Average number of co-investors   3
> - Average size of equity taken   20%

CHARACTERISTICS OF INCOME SEEKING ANGELS

Our study suggests that while the personal characteristics of Income Seeking Angels are very similar to those of the other individual Angel types, they are considerably less wealthy and less entrepreneurial than both Entrepreneur Angels and Wealth Maximising Angels. As is the case for most individual Business Angels, Income Seeking Angels tend to be almost exclusively male, middle-aged, well-educated and active.

Income Seeking Angels are very different from the other individual Angel types in terms of their financial and business backgrounds. Only a quarter of them have a net worth (excluding principal residence) in excess of £200 000, with a third of them worth less than £100 000. This presents a clear contrast with the wealth of the two other active individual Angel types, both of whom have an average net worth of more than £1 million. Income Seeking Angels have higher "relative" incomes, in that 48 per cent of them earn more than £50 000 a year. Income Seeking Angels were also significantly less

---

Profile of Income Seeking Angels

- Average age   48 years
- Gender (percentage of males)   98%
- Education (percentage of university graduates)   47%
- Training (percentage with technical/professional training)   49%
- Sport (percentage that plays competitive sport)   70%

---

entrepreneurial than other Angel types during their own business career. On average they have founded only 0.4 substantial new businesses (businesses employing more than five people or with a turnover of more than £1 million), and nearly two-thirds have not founded any substantial new businesses. In this regard they are clearly very different from the other Angel types.

Financial and Business Backgrounds of Income Seeking Angels

- Net worth (excluding residence) > £100 000   65%
- Net worth (excluding residence) > £200 000   25%
- Annual income > £50 000   48%
- Number of substantial businesses founded   0.4 businesses

PREFERENCES AND EXPECTATIONS OF INCOME SEEKING ANGELS

A roughly equal number of Income Seeking Angels choose to invest to create a job/income for themselves (44 per cent) as invest for financial returns (47 per cent). In this regard the investment reasons of these Angels resemble those of the Wealth Maximising Angels. It is interesting to note that only 18 per cent of Income Seeking Angels choose to invest for fun/satisfaction. This is considerably less than for each of the other Angel types and suggests that for Income Seeking Angels investing is a very serious business. This is hardly surprising given the dramatically lower levels of funds they have available for investing. Despite the fact that this group does not choose to invest for fun, more than three-quarters of them say they enjoy making their informal investments.

Each of the Angel groups pointed to their impression of the founder/ manager of the venture as being their primary investment criterion. In the case of Income Seeking Angels more than 55 cent cite this as their most important criterion. These Angels appear to be successful in their appraisal of founder/managers because in almost 85 per cent of their deals they have a good relationship with the venture founder/manager. It is noteworthy that for more than a third of Income Seeking Angels the most important factor is that they have experience in the industry sector in which the venture is located (34 per cent). This value is higher than for the other individual Angel types and may well reflect the desire of these Angels to take on a formal management position in the ventures. Income Seeking Angels tend to feel the greatest non-financial contribution that they can make to the ventures they finance is to take up formal management positions in them.

In general, Income Seeking Angels do not see venture location as being a particularly important investment criterion. On average the ventures they support are about 80 miles from their place of work. A substantial minority, (one-fifth) of Income Seeking Angels would only consider investment proposals located within 50 miles of their place of work, while another quarter feel restricted to investing within 100 miles. The fact that this number wish to invest in their locality may well stem from a desire of these Angels to be actively involved in the day-to-day running of the ventures they finance.

Friends/family represent the largest single source of deals for Income Seeking Angels. More of these Angels use business introduction services as a source for their deals than any of the other Angel types. These Angels are not satisfied with the current quality of the investment proposals they receive. Figure 6.1 shows that nearly two-thirds of Income Seeking Angels would increase their investment activity if they could have better access to suitable investment proposals. Such concern about the lack of quality deal proposals

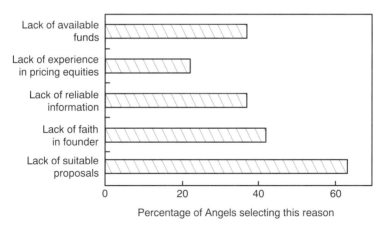

Figure 6.1 Reasons Cited by Income Seeking Angels for not Making Informal Investments

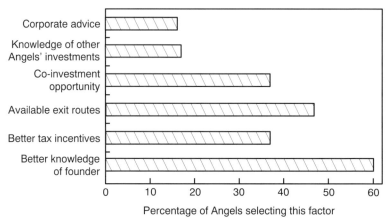

Figure 6.2   Factors that would Encourage Income Seeking Angels to Increase their Investments Activity

mirrors the experience of all the other Angel types. It is also important to note that almost 40 per cent of Income Seeking Angels feel that their current investment activity is restricted by a lack of available funds. Given the relatively low net worth of Income Seeking Angels, this restriction is not surprising. Indeed, only 44 per cent of these Angels have more than £50 000 available for further investment. Only Entrepreneur Angels (32 per cent) resemble Income Seeking Angels in citing a shortage of funds as restricting their investment activity.

Almost three-quarters of Income Seeking Angels feel that their investment activity is likely to increase in the next five years. There are, however, a number of factors that would encourage them to further increase their investment activity, summarised in Figure 6.2. Most Income Seeking Angels would like to be able to gain a greater understanding of the founder/manager whose venture they are being asked to finance, and almost half of them want to see more clearly available exit routes for their investments.

NON-FINANCIAL CONTRIBUTION OF INCOME SEEKING ANGELS

In our research we were interested in the role that each of the Angel types takes up in the ventures they finance. In particular we sought to examine whether the Angels who indicated that they were investing in unquoted ventures to create a job/income for themselves made a different sort of non-financial contribution to those who were investing for financial gain or for fun/satisfaction. Figure 6.3 summarises the principal non-financial contributions

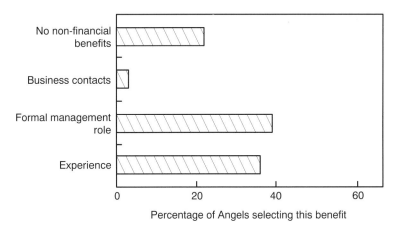

Figure 6.3   Non-financial Benefits Income Seeking Angels feel they bring to Ventures

of Income Seeking Angels. The largest number of these Angels (39 per cent) feel that their greatest non-financial contribution is to take up a formal management position in the ventures, although almost as many (36 per cent) point to their general experience and expertise as representing their principal contribution. The management contribution is cited more often by Income Seeking Angels than by Entrepreneur and Wealth Maximising Angels, and reinforces the view that these Angels invest to create a job/income for themselves as well as for financial returns.

In general, Income Seeking Angels visit their ventures slightly more than once a week, and telephone slightly more frequently than that. Surprisingly, this level of contact is below that of Wealth Maximising Angels. However, it is difficult to be certain exactly what a once weekly visit or telephone call involves.

SUMMARY FOR INCOME SEEKING ANGELS

Income Seeking Angels are active individual investors who have made one or two low level investments over the past three years. The key points to remember about Income Seeking Angels are:

- They are well-off, but not as wealthy as the other Angel types.
- They make their investments both for financial gain and to generate a job/income for themselves; they may well wish to take a full-time position in the start-up, and with their experience this may be an attractive option.

Income Seeking Angel Example

STEVEN HUNTER*

Age: 45; Location: Devon

As a native of Devon, Steven Hunter returned to Devon three years ago to buy a shareholding in a small unquoted landscaping company, which now employs him full-time. Although his history is slightly more entrepreneurial than that of most Income Seeking Angels, Steven clearly does fit the mould: his primary investment motive was to generate an income and a job for himself. Although there are fewer entrepreneurial investment opportunities in the south-west area of England, Steven's patience paid off when he discovered this particular investment opportunity within driving distance of his home. Steven is now actively involved in building this business into a large and competitive player in the landscaping market. So far his efforts seem to have paid off.

Born and bred in Devon, Steven finished school with nine O levels and three A levels. After gaining his OND in business studies, he became an articled clerk in Bristol. With more training over the subsequent five years, he became a certified accountant and advised businesses—thus "learning from the business mistakes of others!" In 1982 he founded his own firm, a specialist computer contract agency. This proved to be quite profitable—so much so that he sold it for a sizeable gain in 1987 and stayed on with the new parent company until 1991. Frustrated by the bureaucracy of the parent firm, Steven again started a new firm, this time a revenue collection service. After also growing this firm quite successfully, Steven sold the company and went into semi-retirement. He travelled Eastern Europe quite extensively and upon his return to the UK decided to find a suitable investment opportunity so that he could again enjoy the entrepreneurial process of building up a small company.

Having made some unquoted investments in the past, Steven was not new to the role of Business Angel. While considering various investment opportunities, Steven has two main prerequisites for investment. First, the business must have great potential. He looks for a business with a sizeable marketplace, strong sales potential and an idea that "must be able to fly". Secondly, "the entrepreneurs must be enthusiastic and be committed to the venture". Since he wished to be very actively involved in the firm, the compatibility and the trustworthiness of the people was a critical factor in Steven's investment decision. In the investment he made, the chemistry between the

---

* A pseudonym was used to protect the anonymity of the Business Angel. All other data is factual and has been taken from a 90-minute interview Mark van Osnabrugge held with the Business Angel on 13 February 1996.

entrepreneurs and him was outstanding: "The trust and reliance was 100 per cent."

In his search for an investment opportunity, Steven was deterred by many factors. In particular, he shied away from high-tech companies (most of which he didn't fully understand). He says: "Without a background in high-tech, there is no use competing with high-tech entrepreneurs who know the business inside and out." Other factors that deterred him were firms without a distinct market niche capable of growth, and those without some type of competitive edge over the competition. The particular product of the company was of little concern for him, as long as the fundamentals of the firm looked promising.

With Steven's help, the landscaping firm has trebled in size over the last three years since his financial investment. With an intended time commitment of 5–7 years, Steven expects to build up this firm for a few more years, before he considers other entrepreneurial investment opportunities.

7
The Wealth Maximising Angel

This group of active Angel investors comprise private individuals who have made several investments in new and growing ventures. Wealth Maximising Angels tend to be very wealthy, without being quite as rich as Entrepreneur Angels, and make their investments predominantly for financial gain. This chapter examines the investment activity, the personal and business backgrounds, the investment preferences and expectations, and the non-financial contribution of Wealth Maximising Angels.

INVESTMENT ACTIVITY OF WEALTH MAXIMISING ANGELS

Wealth Maximising Angels tend to have made a couple of large investments over the past three years. On average these Angels invest £131 000 in 2.1 ventures during this period. While a number invest above this level, we found only 8 per cent of these Angels invest more than £200 000 in unquoted ventures. The investment activity of Wealth Maximising Angels is significantly lower than that of Entrepreneur Angels and Corporate Angels, both in terms of the number of investments made and the level of funds invested. However, this group makes more frequent investments and provides higher levels of funds than Income Seeking Angels.

Overall Investment Activity of Wealth Maximising Angels

- Average number of investments   2.1
- Total amount invested   £131 000
- Percentage investing more than £200 000   8%

Our study examined 137 separate investment deals involving 68 different Wealth Maximising Angels. On average, Wealth Maximising Angels were found to have invested £54 000 in each deal. Typically only about 40 per cent of this sum was provided in the initial round of investment. This level of investment is clearly well below that provided by Entrepreneur and Corporate Angels but represents more than double the typical amount invested by Income Seeking Angels. Wealth Maximising Angels tend to acquire substantial minority shareholdings in the ventures they back. The average size of the stakeholding for these investors is just over 30 per cent. Only about 30 per cent of these Angels have a preference for majority holdings; 60 per cent of these Angels have a preference for co-investment and on average their deals involve 2.5 other investors (including the venture founder/manager).

A Typical Wealth Maximising Angel Deal

- Average total amount invested   £54 000
- Average initial amount invested   £21 000
- Average number of rounds of investment   1.75
- Average number of co-investors   2.5

CHARACTERISTICS OF WEALTH MAXIMISING ANGELS

Our research suggests that while the personal characteristics of Wealth Maximising Angels closely resemble those of the other individual Angel types, they are considerably wealthier than Income Seeking Angels, and significantly less entrepreneurial than Entrepreneur Angels. Although Wealth Maximising Angels share the characteristics of all Business Angels in that they tend to be male, middle-aged, active and well educated, these Angels were found to be slightly younger than the Entrepreneur Angels, and to have received a higher level of formal education than both of the other types of individual Angels.

There are quite clear distinctions between the financial and business backgrounds of Wealth Maximising Angels and those of other active Angels. While these individuals are not quite as wealthy as Entrepreneur Angels, they are nonetheless very wealthy. More than 80 per cent of the group are worth more than £500 000 (excluding principal residence), with half that number again being worth over £1 million. Almost 40 per cent continue to earn more than £100 000 a year. This level of wealth and income sets Wealth Maximising Angels apart from Income Seeking Angels, the majority of whom are worth less than £200 000, and have incomes of less than £50 000 a year. As is the case

Profile of Wealth Maximising Angels

- Average age   48 years
- Gender (percentage of males)   98%
- Education (percentage of university graduates)   57%
- Training (percentage with technical/professional training)   44%
- Sport (percentage who play competitive sports)   71%

for all Business Angels, this wealth was almost predominantly self-made. However, more of these Angels earned their wealth through inheritance than was the case for any of the other Angel types.

Financial and Business Backgrounds of Wealth Maximising Angels

- Net worth (excluding residence) > £500 000   82%
- Net worth (excluding residence) > £1 000 000   43%
- Annual income > £100 000   38%
- Number of substantial businesses founded   1.3

While Wealth Maximising Angels appear to mirror Entrepreneur Angels in terms of their wealth and income, there are very clear differences between these groups in terms of entrepreneurial background. On average Wealth Maximising Angels have founded 1.3 substantial new businesses during the course of their own business careers. This figure is considerably higher than the average of 0.4 for Income Seeking Angels, but dramatically lower than the figure of 4.0 for Entrepreneur Angels. This thesis suggests that the experience and enthusiasm Entrepreneur Angels had for entrepreneurship during their own careers is at least partly responsible for their greater informal investment activity.

PREFERENCES AND EXPECTATIONS OF WEALTH MAXIMISING ANGELS

Wealth Maximising Angels invest for financial returns and to create a job/income for themselves, while the most important investment criterion is their impression of the founder/manager of the venture. Almost half (46 per cent) of these investors choose to invest in unquoted ventures because they expect the financial return to exceed those offered by quoted shares. A large number of these investors, 43 per cent, choose to make Angel investments because of the opportunity to create a job/income for themselves. In this regard the Wealth Maximising Angels mirror Income Seeking Angels who also cite this job/income factor as an important investment reason. However, almost a third of this group point to fun and satisfaction as their principal reason for choosing to invest in unquoted ventures and this reflects the investment reasons of Entrepreneur Angels. Wealth Maximising Angels tend to derive less satisfaction from their investments than either Entrepreneur or Income Seeking Angels, with over 70 per cent indicating that their experience has been positive. In fact, only Corporate Angels appear to be less satisfied with their investment activity.

As with all of the other Angel types, Wealth Maximising Angels cite their impression of the founder/manager to be the most important investment criterion (60 per cent). More than a quarter (26 per cent) of these Angels look to invest in industries in which they have some personal experience. While this value is not as high as the 34 per cent attributed by Income Seeking Angels, or the 27 per cent by Corporate Angels, it is higher than the 19 per cent indicated by Entrepreneur Angels. The higher importance that these Angel groups place on their own sector experience, allied to their greater desire to create a job/income for themselves (43 per cent), suggests that Wealth Maximising, Income Seeking and Corporate Angels are more likely to take on a day-to-day management role in their ventures than Entrepreneur Angels. Indeed, when the actual non-financial contribution of Wealth Maximising Angels is examined, a substantially larger number are found to have taken on a formal or full-time position than was the case for Entrepreneurial Angels.

The existing literature on informal investment has consistently pointed to venture location as being an important investment criterion for Business Angels. The responses of the Angels who participated in this research do not support this idea. Even though all the respondents were free to rank jointly, only 4 per cent of Wealth Maximising Angels ranked venture location as their most important investment criterion. The average distance of the ventures from the place of work of Wealth Maximising Angels is 114 miles, while over 40 per cent of these Angels indicated that they would be willing to invest in ventures more than 200 miles away. Less than 20 per cent of Wealth Maximising Angels felt restricted to investing within 50 miles of their place of work.

More than three-quarters of Wealth Maximising Angels feel that their current investment activity is being restricted by a lack of suitable business proposals (see Figure 7.1). This lack of access to quality investment proposals is the single biggest factor restricting the investment activity of all the Angel types. Friends/family represent the largest source of information for the current investments of Wealth Maximising Angels. Business introduction services account for only a small percentage of the current deals for this group of angels. It is clear that the investment activity of the Angel types could be increased by improving the quality of the deal flow between entrepreneurs and investors.

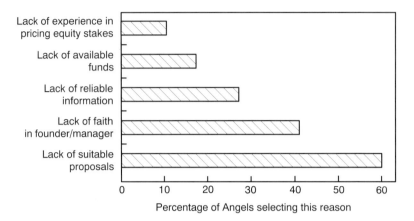

Figure 7.1 Reasons Cited by Wealth Maximising Angels for not Making Informal Investments

It is also interesting to note that a significantly lower percentage of Wealth Maximising Angels cite a lack of available funds as restricting their investment than was the case for Entrepreneur Angels. This suggests that Wealth Maximising Angels have the funds available for further investment and would invest if the deal flow problems could be overcome. Over 82 per cent of Wealth Maximising Angels would like to increase their investment activity over the next five years. Exactly half of these Angels have more than £100 000 available for further informal investment. This is considerably more than that available for Income Seeking Angels, but a great deal less than the available portfolio of Entrepreneur Angels.

Wealth Maximising Angels would invest more if they could gain a better understanding of the founder/manager of the ventures that approach them for finance. Unlike Entrepreneur Angels, better tax incentives are not a major factor.

Wealth Maximising Angels differ from other Angel types in that nearly three-quarters of them would be encouraged to increase their investment activity if they could either invest jointly with more experienced investors, or have access to the knowledge of these investors. Perhaps a forum such as the Oxfordshire Investment Opportunity Network (profiled in Chapter 14), which brings groups of private investors together, could provide such a medium.

NON-FINANCIAL CONTRIBUTION OF WEALTH MAXIMISING ANGELS

The vast majority of Wealth Maximising Angels feel that they bring substantially more than just capital to the ventures they finance. Almost half of these

Table 7.1 Principal Non-financial Benefit Wealth Maximising Angels Feel they Bring to Ventures

Benefit	Value
Experience/expertise	49%
Formal management role/employment	32%
Business contacts	3%
No non-financial benefit	15%

angels suggest that the general business experience and expertise they bring to a venture represents their greatest non-financial contribution (see Table 7.1). This is significantly more than was found to be the case for Entrepreneur Angels, and more than that indicated by Income Seeking Angels. Approximately a third of Wealth Maximising Angels cite a formal management role, or full-time employment of some kind, as their principal non-financial contribution. This is less than the almost 40 per cent indicated by Income Seeking Angels, but nonetheless highlights the desire of these Angels to be involved to some extent in the day-to-day operations of their ventures.

Bearing in mind that almost a third of Wealth Maximising Angels view some sort of formal management role to be beneficial to the ventures they finance, it is interesting to examine the degree of actual contact they have with their ventures. This research found that on average, Wealth Maximising Angels visit the businesses they support 67 times a year and telephone them on 86 occasions during the same period. This level of contact is higher than that for any of the other Angel types. In particular it is surprising that it exceeds the level of contact made by Income Seeking Angels. However, this level of analysis is an extremely blunt instrument, in that the type of activity being carried out on each visit, and the sort of telephone discussions being held, cannot be determined.

SUMMARY FOR WEALTH MAXIMISING ANGELS

This group of active Angel investors comprise wealthy private individuals who have made several investments in new and growing ventures.

The key points to remember about Wealth Maximising Angels are:

- Not surprisingly, they tend to be very wealthy though without being quite as rich as Entrepreneur Angels.
- They make their investments primarily for financial gain.

Wealth Maximising Angel Example

BILL GRINTER*

Age: 37; Location: London

With a successful entrepreneurial career in the computer industry behind him, Bill Grinter now uses the experience he has gained over the years to invest in small, risky start-up companies, similar to the one he started. Using the substantial financial gains he earned from the sale of his own firm, Bill and his business partner have set up an investment company to invest, primarily for financial gain, in an array of small firms. Since they started investing four years ago, they have made seven unquoted investments in businesses "which they felt good about and will make them money". None has yet been exited, some look lacklustre, but most are showing promising growth.

Bill started his entrepreneurial career in the early 1980s. After completing his O levels in "the usual subjects" (Maths, English, Physics and Biology), Bill took a job as a computer operator. Looking for more opportunity, he became a salesman selling large printing machines to industrial clients. This also proved limited, so he joined Olivetti as a computer salesman. After a few months with them, he noticed that Olivetti was shifting its sales focus from direct sales to third party sales. This meant that as the computer industry was growing, more sophisticated equipment was entering an inexperienced dealer network, which only a few years before had been primarily selling typewriters. Spotting this market opportunity and wishing to make use of his computer skills, Bill became a computer dealer in 1983. With hard work and his computer expertise, Bill's dealership expanded rapidly and in 1989 he sold the business for a substantial gain.

To ensure a smooth hand-over, Bill agreed to stay with the firm for another two years, after which he started his investment firm in early 1992. In this manner, he is again self-employed, giving him "freedom and fun" and the time to use his "entrepreneurial skills to help firms he has invested in". With a handful of unquoted investments, Bill and his partner try to be as actively involved as their time permits, but he admits that sometimes he is a little frustrated that he now is the "outsider [investor], rather than the entrepreneur running the firm 'hands on' on a daily basis".

In selecting firms to finance, Bill uses two main guidelines. First, "does the business appeal to him as a pure business?" If there is nothing unique about the company's approach or if it "does not offer something unique to help it

---

* A pseudonym was used to protect the anonymity of the Business Angel. All other data is factual and has been taken from a 90-minute interview Mark van Osnabrugge held with the Business Angel on 23 February 1996.

succeed, a competitive advantage of some sort", then he is not interested. Secondly, "after meeting the people [entrepreneurs], do you believe in them? Does it feel right?" Bill admits that this is rather subjective, but feels that the personal relationship with the entrepreneur(s) is often critical to success. In his last investment, in a film production company, he was particularly drawn to the venture because the entrepreneur was someone he could "trust". Bill states that "this particular entrepreneur was enthusiastic, straightforward, and honest—these are the building blocks of a strong relationship".

Bill realises that these small entrepreneurial firms are "high risk", but he is a true "believer in new companies". Recently he helped a small firm gain finance, which was a rewarding experience for him since "any small firm has a hard time getting money, but quite often they deserve the chance to prove themselves".

Wealth Maximising Angel Example

TOM BRAKERT*

Age: 59; Location: Sussex

As one of the most successful and more experienced Business Angels interviewed during this research, Tom Brakert has used his varied business experience to invest in small unquoted firms. Having made a substantial amount of money from establishing a number of his own firms, Tom has spent the last few years investing full time in an array of investments, in particular young entrepreneurial firms. Since these companies are usually high risk, Tom tries to keep only about 10–15 per cent of his invested capital in them. Although he states that his main motive for making unquoted investments is financial gains, he also expresses the joy he gets from being part of the entrepreneurial process. "If I lose all the money that I've invested in these small firms, it really won't affect my lifestyle, or future plans, in a significant way. Don't get me wrong: it would be disappointing for me as an investor, but at least I would have tried something I enjoy—helping small firms." Looking at Tom's track record, few (if any) of his investments have been disappointing.

Tom is a self-made man, whose entrepreneurial successes enabled him to pursue the investor role he now enjoys. His history is quite typical of that of many Business Angels.

After finishing secondary school, Tom spent five years in the Royal Air Force as a pilot and air traffic controller. At the age of 22, he joined the Cadbury Group and worked in sales and marketing. During the subsequent ten years, Tom held "ten different jobs", gaining different business experiences in each one of them. Then, at the age of 32, Tom started his own business selling shop equipment. After this proved to be a success, he sold the firm and started another, which sold cooling cabinets. This company too was sold and this allowed Tom to start his third business selling office products. After years of growth, this firm was bought out by FiloFax. From this sale Tom made a substantial profit, enough money to enable him to become a full-time investor in entrepreneurial firms.

Although he is now approaching 60, Tom has no desire to slow down, retire, or stop investing. He still likes to be actively involved. All his unquoted investments must be able to render him the opportunity for "hands-on involvement" so that he can "contribute his skills" and make use of all his industry contacts. Tom feels that his commercial business skills and general

---

* A pseudonym was used to protect the anonymity of the Business Angel. All other data is factual and has been taken from a 90-minute interview Mark van Osnabrugge held with the Business Angel on 29 March 1996.

business knowledge are his greatest business strengths and therefore usually doesn't invest in firms that are "too technical" or those he doesn't fully understand. He prefers companies that are in a market niche and offer something unique, and if they don't, they must offer the possibility of making their product or service unique.

Like most investors, Tom is careful to assess the riskiness of potential investments. He elects to shy away from those firms with high risks and high potential returns. Tom's approach entails only funding firms with medium risk and medium returns, with an average compound return on investment of 30 per cent. Although he usually doesn't conduct an extensive overview of the financials, he believes that if the business is fundamentally sound, the financials will also turn out to be promising.

Tom's most recent investment was in a small company that produces construction tools. After careful evaluation of the entrepreneurs, products and the market, Tom and two co-investors bought almost 40 per cent of the company. In this instance, co-investing was his preference: "There is a certain comfort in going in as part of a team."

Despite his sizeable portfolio of unquoted investments, Tom is still looking for more good entrepreneurial opportunities. For him, it is clearly something more than the financial gains that drives his desire to invest in unquoted ventures.

8
The Latent Angel

This chapter focuses on the group of inactive Angels who have made one or more informal investments in the past, but who have remained inactive for at least the past three years. These Latent Angels are very wealthy self-made private individuals, with substantial funds available to invest, who are now interested in making informal investments. Of all the Angel types, Latent Angels are the most concerned with venture location, and they cite the lack of suitable locally based proposals as having restricted their investment activity.

The financial and business characteristics of this kind of inactive investor are similar to those of the Wealth Maximising Angels. In this chapter we examine the expected investment activity, the personal and business characteristics, and the investment preferences of Latent Angels.

EXPECTED INVESTMENT ACTIVITY OF LATENT ANGELS

Latent Angels are distinct from active Angels in that they have made no informal investments in the past three years, but differ from Virgin Angels because they have made this form of investment at some time. The historic investments of Latent Angels were not of interest to our research and no details of their investment activity from that period were obtained. This study does seek to discover the desire of these Angels to invest informally again and tries to estimate the size of their likely investment portfolio. It also looks at why these individuals have not invested in unquoted ventures during the past three years, and is especially concerned with examining any factors that would encourage them to invest informally again.

Latent Angels are very interested in making informal investments again. We found that 63 per cent of them expected to make one or more investments over the next five years, while only 14 per cent thought it unlikely that they would invest in unquoted ventures during that period. Latent Angels have substantial funds at their disposal for this form of investment. Only a quarter of this group have less than £50 000 available, while more than half have more than £100 000 and more than 10 per cent have more than £1 million available for informal investments. This level of funds is significantly higher than that available to Virgin Angels; indeed, it is apparent that some of these Angels have very extensive resources. Consequently it appears very unlikely that the current investment activity of Latent Angels has been curtailed by a lack of financial resources—our research found that only a quarter of these Angels attributed their inactivity to a lack of available funds. Table 8.1 compares the amount of funds Latent Angels have available, compared with Virgin Angels and Active Angels.

The most common factor restricting the current investment activity of Latent Angels is the lack of suitable business proposals (see Figure 8.1). Over three-quarters of these Angels point to a shortage of quality investment proposals as being the principal reason behind their decision not to invest and, indeed, over three-quarters explicitly stated that they would have invested in one or more ventures over the past three years if there had been more suitable

Table 8.1 Level of Funds Available to Latent Angels for Informal Investment

Size of available portfolio	£50 000	£50 000– £100 000	£100 000– £200 000	£200 000– £500 000	£500 000– £1 million	< £1 million
Latent Angels	28%	17%	28%	8%	6%	11%
Virgin Angels	38%	32%	19%	8%	3%	–
Active Angels*	24%	27%	19%	17%	4%	7%

* These figures refer only to the funds that active Angels have still available for investment—they exclude existing Angel investments.

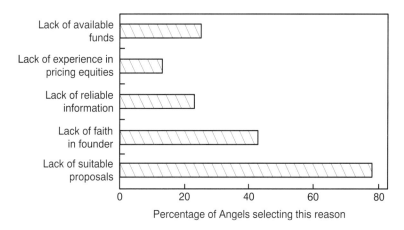

Figure 8.1 Reasons Cited by Latent Angels for not Making Informal Investments

proposals available to them. These problems of information transfer in the informal venture market appear to affect all Business Angels. But it appears that this problem impacts particularly severely on Latent Angels because their level of concern (78 per cent) is higher than for those for the other Angel types (Virgin Angels (65 per cent), active Angels (70 per cent)). The inability of Latent Angels to locate suitable business proposals is especially unfortunate because they clearly have high levels of funds available.

Latent Angels are also concerned with the personality and trustworthiness of the founder or manager of the venture seeking finance: 43 per cent of Latent Angels point to a lack of faith in these founder/managers as the principal reason preventing them from investing in unquoted ventures. This represents a significantly greater concern than that found for Virgin Angels, but mirrors the concern that active Angels have with the founder/managers of the ventures they finance. Other hindrances cited by Latent Angels include a lack of reliable information (23 per cent) and a lack of experience in pricing equity stakes (13 per cent). It is also interesting to note that the proportion of Latent Angels who point to a lack of funds as being the principal factor curtailing their investment activity (25 per cent) is considerably higher than that for Virgin Angels, despite the fact that Latent Angels appear to have larger investment portfolios. In this regard Latent Angels are similar to active Angels, slightly more than a quarter of whom feel their investment activity is restricted by a lack of financial resources.

Latent Angels are significantly more concerned with the proximity of the venture to their home or place of work than the active Angel types. The majority of Latent Angels will not consider proposals for ventures located more than 100 miles away, and about a quarter restrict themselves to proposals for ventures located within 50 miles of their place of work. Undoubtedly this desire to restrict their investment to local ventures reduces the pool of quality proposals available to Latent Angels.

Almost two-thirds of Latent Angels believe that they would be more likely to make informal investments if they could gain a better knowledge of, or trust in, the venture founders who approach them for finance (see Figure 8.2). Latent Angels would also be encouraged to invest if they could see more clearly available exit routes available to them. The other principal factors which would help Latent Angels to become active Angels are the opportunity to co-invest with more experienced investors, and better tax incentives. The desire for co-investment reflects the desire of the survey respondents generally to involve other Angels in their ventures. Latent Angels are less concerned with tax incentives than the other Angel types. With regard to the government's recent Enterprise Investment Scheme (EIS) initiative only about a quarter feel it was more likely to encourage informal investment than its predecessor, the Business Expansion Scheme (BES), while 40 per cent feel it will actually discourage future investments.

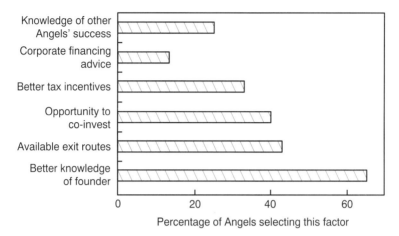

Figure 8.2 Factors that would Encourage Latent Angels to Increase their Investment Activity

CHARACTERISTICS OF LATENT ANGELS

Latent Angels tend to be very wealthy, highly educated men who are slightly older than the typical Virgin Angel or active Angel investor. In most respects their financial and business backgrounds resemble those of the Wealth Maximising Angels.

The Latent Angels identified by this survey were exclusively male and were found to be slightly older (50 years) than Virgin Angels (46 years) and active Angels (48 years). Latent Angels are also very well educated, with the majority having reached a high level of formal education and/or professional or technical training: 70 per cent of them have been to university and over a quarter have postgraduate degrees, while almost half of them have professional or technical qualifications. These Angels are active people and three-quarters of them regularly participate in competitive sport. The personal characteristics of all the participants in this study were remarkably similar and as a result the different Angel types share many common personal characteristics. In this regard Latent Angels are very similar in biographical terms to each of the other Angel types.

Our research found Latent Angels to be significantly wealthier and more entrepreneurial than the other type of inactive Angel, the Virgin Angel. Indeed, in terms of net worth and annual income Latent Angels are similar to active Angels generally, and in particular to the Wealth Maximising Angel. More than half of Latent Angels are worth over £500 000 (excluding their principal residence), while over 40 per cent of them are worth more than £1 million (see Table 8.2). As with most of the Angel types the wealth of

Profile of Latent Angels

- Average age   50 years
- Gender (percentage of males)   100%
- Education (percentage of university graduates)   70%
- Training (percentage with technical/professional training)   48%
- Sport (percentage that plays competitive sport)   75%

Latent Angels is predominantly self-made—only 8 per cent cite inheritance as their principal source of wealth. Almost three-quarters of them continue to have annual incomes in excess of £50 000. Clearly, Angels in this group are very wealthy and they appear to have substantial financial resources available to invest in suitable informal investment proposals.

Table 8.2   The Net Worth of Latent Angels

Net worth (excluding principal residence)	£50 000	£50 000– £100 000	£100 000– £200 000	£200 000– £500 000	£500 000– £1 million	< £1 million
Latent Angels	5%	–	11%	32%	11%	42%
Virgin Angels	12%	11%	18%	23%	11%	25%
Active Angels	3%	8%	16%	18%	20%	37%

Financial and Business Backgrounds of Latent Angels

- Net worth (excluding residence) > £500 000   53%
- Net worth (excluding residence) > £1 000 000   42%
- Annual income > £50 000   74%
- Number of substantial businesses founded   1.5

   This study has consistently held that the entrepreneurial background of Business Angels is an important influence on their informal investment activity. On average, Latent Angels were found to have started 1.5 substantial new businesses (businesses employing more than five people or with a turnover of more than £1 million) during their own business careers. This represents a significantly greater level of entrepreneurship than that of Virgin Angels and a similar degree to that of active Angels generally. However, when it is compared to the different types of active Angel, it is found to be very similar to the average 1.3 businesses founded by Wealth Maximising Angels, and significantly lower than the average of four businesses for Entrepreneur Angels.

INVESTMENT PREFERENCES OF LATENT ANGELS

Our research suggests that Latent Angels are looking to make informal investments to earn high financial returns and to create a job/income for themselves. The most important criteria for Latent Angels when assessing proposals are the personalities of the venture founder, their own industry sector experience, and the geographic proximity of the venture. In terms of structuring an investment deal, Latent Angels are more likely to take a majority stake and less likely to co-invest than most active Angels.

Current British and American research (KPMG, 1992; Mason and Harrison, 1993; Wetzel and Freear, 1993; van Osnabrugge, 1998) argues that Business Angels invest predominantly for financial benefit. The Latent Angels identified in this study were interested in making informal investments principally for financial returns—almost 60 per cent indicated that the reason they would choose to back an unquoted venture would be because they expect the returns to be higher than those on quoted ventures. Forty per cent of Latent Angels are seeking an informal investment to create either a job or a regular income for themselves. This is significantly lower than the 50 per cent of Virgin Angels who cite this as their principal reason for looking to invest in unquoted ventures (see Table 8.3). However, the focus of Latent Angels on returns and on job/income is considerably higher than that for active Angels. It appears that fun and/or satisfaction do not represent major investment reasons for these individuals. Only 22 per cent of them cite this as their principal investment reason, whereas 29 per cent of active Angels do so.

In assessing business proposals the most important criteria for Latent Angels are their impression of the founder/manager (49 per cent), the personal experience of Latent Angels in the industry sector where the prospective venture is to be located (28 per cent), and the geographic proximity of the venture to the Angel's place of work (13 per cent). There is no significant difference between the relative importance of the founder/manager and that of personal experience for Latent and active Angels. However, the number of

Table 8.3 The Reasons that Most Attract Latent Angels to Make Informal Investments

Reason	Latent Angels	Active Angels
Expect greater returns than from quoted shares	58%	50%
To create a job/income for themselves	40%	33%
Fun and satisfaction	22%	29%
Sense of social responsibility	5%	4%
Other	8%	7%

Table 8.4 The Maximum Distance from the Place of Work that Angels would Consider Making Informal Investments

Distance	Latent Angels	Active Angels
< 50 miles, or < 1 hour journey time	23%	15%
< 100 miles, or < 2 hours journey time	33%	25%
< 200 miles, or < 3 hours journey time	21%	16%
> 200 miles, or > 3 hours journey time	23%	44%

Table 8.5 Deal Preferences and Expectations of Latent Angels Compared with those of Active Angels

Expectation	Latent Angels	Active Angels
Level of co-investment	40% favour co-investment	52% favour co-investment
Size of share-holding	42% prefer majority stakes	34% prefer majority stakes
Turnover of venture	£2 000 000 (5 years)	£2 600 000 (5 years)
Rate of annual growth	25%	22%
Rate of annual return	17%	19%
Timeframe for exit	6 years	6 years

Latent Angels who consider the geographic location of a venture to be the most important criterion when considering financing a venture is significantly higher than for active Angel investors. In fact, almost a quarter (23 per cent) of these Angels would only consider investing in a venture that is located within 50 miles of their place of work, while 56 per cent of them would want the venture to be within 100 miles. This concern with investing in locally based proposals sets Latent Angels apart from each of the active types of Angels (see Table 8.4).

This research was especially interested in examining the preferences Latent Angels have for the structure and expected performance of their prospective investment deals (see Table 8.5, which makes comparisons with active Angels). We found that Latent Angels are more likely to take majority stakes and less likely to co-invest than active Angels. Also, Latent Angels tend to be interested in slightly smaller businesses than other Angel types. However, in terms of expected levels of growth and return, and timeframe for exit there is virtually no difference between Latent and active Angels, or between Latent and Virgin Angels.

SUMMARY FOR LATENT ANGELS

These inactive investors we call Latent Angels are interested in making informal investments and have considerable resources available to do so. They are restricted from making this form of investment by a lack of suitable, locally based proposals. The key points to remember concerning Latent Angels are:

- A better knowledge of the founder/management team of the prospective venture, and more clearly available exit routes would encourage these Angels to invest again.
- Latent Angels are wealthier and more entrepreneurial than Virgin Angels and are more concerned with venture location than any of the other Angels.

Latent Angel Example

RICHARD BARGE*

Age: 55; Location: Oxfordshire

After successfully exiting a firm that he built from scratch, Richard decided that, instead of starting another venture himself he would invest in a small unquoted firm that was just starting. He really wanted the opportunity to use his business expertise to help an entrepreneur build up a small firm. Unbeknown to Richard, he was taking on a Business Angel role. In 1984, he invested in three unquoted start-ups, in the hope that one might be successful. One certainly was and Richard is a director at that firm today. Since then he has not made any more Business Angel investments, although he continues to keep an eye out for investment opportunities.

Born in West Sussex, Richard went to public school in Kent where his main interests were science and English. After school he had to satisfy his national service obligation, so he volunteered for the Navy at the age of 18 and had 24 postings in the subsequent two years. Then, at 20, he went up to Oxford University to read Physics. There he became one of his college's most successful rowers, setting an unprecedented record: 18 straight months of victories without defeat. Upon completion of his degree, he joined British Oxygen as a Commercial Trainee, and after a year of training he was qualified to "swim through all the bureaucracy and utilise the methods of selling in a monopoly!" With little hope of promotion, Richard resigned three years later and spent the next year "finding himself" and enjoying a carefree life. But the peaceful life did not suit him, so at the age of 27, he joined Anfield, a computer bureau which was a "laundry for firms' invoices". There he learned the basics of computing, which was to serve him well later.

After three years of computer work, Richard joined Blackwells, a jobbing firm in London, where he was market maker in oils. As principals in the oil market, they bought and sold for their own account, and assumed considerable risks on some of those transactions. After a few bad turns, the firm had to merge with an outsider firm and after seven years with the firm Richard changed concentrations and became a consultant to the stock exchange. After a few years there, Richard finally decided to follow his entrepreneurial instincts and left the business with a substantial amount in financial resources.

In 1977 he started his own computer company, which catered to all the computer needs of the member firms of the exchange. This proved to have a

---

* A pseudonym was used to protect the anonymity of the Business Angel. All other data is factual and has been taken from an interview Mark van Osnabrugge held with the Business Angel on 27 January 1997.

limited up-side, so after three years he changed the focus of the firm and became a selling agent for Norsk Data, a Norwegian computer maker. Soon he was bringing in £1 million projects, such as supplying all the computer needs to the JET (nuclear fusion) project and making an annual £500 000 profit. But in 1983 Richard became discontent with the technological innovation of the products he was representing and decided to resign from the company that he had started and grown.

Thus, in 1984 Richard found himself sitting in an Oxford library looking through business introduction service magazines in the hope of finding a local unquoted start-up venture to fund. To diversify his risk, he ended up investing in three, of which one collapsed almost straight away, one remained stagnant, and one grew considerably. This successful firm was a manufacturer of electrical products and has provided Richard not only with daily employment for the last 12 years, but also the challenges of the entrepreneurial process. The company now has £8 million in annual sales and this is increasing rapidly.

Although Richard would like to once more grow a small firm from a greenfield site to a successful large firm, he does not have the financial liquidity to do so. Since his firm is still unquoted, it is extremely difficult for Richard to get his money out of it. Thus, he "remains in a position of not being diversified, which is not the most optimal position to be in". But, he is confident that his investment in the firm will continue to grow and hopes that when the firm does go public, his liquidity problems will be a thing of the past. But even financial non-liquidity has not stopped Richard's entrepreneurial streak: he recently invested in two unquoted firms trading on the Alternative Investment Market (AIM) and the Ofex market.

As a successful entrepreneur and Business Angel, Richard's past actions have painted a fine line between these two distinctive groups. Although in research terms we might consider Richard a Latent Angel (since he has not invested actively in the last three years), he clearly wishes to continue his active involvement in the field of entrepreneurial finance. Due to his current financial constraints, it might be safe to say that Richard's next consideration of an unquoted investment opportunity might place more weight on possible exit routes. As unrealistic as this may sometimes be with unquoted firms, this might also be something that could entice other Latent Angels to invest.

9
The Virgin Angel

This chapter focuses on Virgin Angels, that group of inactive investors who have not yet made an investment in an unquoted venture. Existing American and British research (Mason and Harrison, 1995; Riding *et al*, 1993; Wetzel and Freear, 1993) suggests that there are many more Virgin Angels than active Angels. For example, Riding *et al* (1993) estimated that there are about 100 000 potential Angels in Canada of which only 3 per cent are currently active. In the British case, Mason and Harrison (1995) claim that if half of the Virgin Angels became active, the total informal venture capital market would grow to ten times the size of the formal venture capital market.

Our research has found Virgin Angels to be private individuals who are looking to provide finance to new or growing businesses, with a view to creating a job or a regular income for themselves, and to earn higher returns than those available on the stock market. Virgin Angels are not as wealthy as active Business Angels and have fewer funds available to invest. However, they do not cite this lack of funds as restricting their investment activity, but instead point to an absence of suitable investment proposals. Virgin Angels represent an exciting opportunity. This chapter looks at the expected investment activity, the personal and business characteristics, and the investment preferences of Virgin Angels.

EXPECTED INVESTMENT ACTIVITY OF VIRGIN ANGELS

Virgin Angels are distinct from each of the other types of Angels profiled in this study in that they have yet to make an investment in unquoted ventures. This group is of particular interest because they have expressed a desire to take the plunge and join the pool of active Angel investors. This chapter looks at this desire of Virgin Angels to become active investors, examines the level of funds they have available for this form of investment, studies the reasons that currently prevent them from investing, and identifies specific factors that would encourage them to invest.

Virgin Angels have a very strong desire to invest in unquoted ventures—almost 90 per cent of this group expect to make one or more informal investments over the next five years. Although the Business Angels and potential Angels who participated in our research were drawn from a convenience sample of likely informal investors, the fact that the pool of active investors is likely to increase by almost a third suggests that the economic potential of this source of small business finance is very large indeed. Furthermore, Virgin Angels have substantial resources available for informal investment. Table 9.1 shows the level of funds Angels have available for this form of investment and compares it with that of active Business Angels. Virgin Angels still have considerable resources at their disposal. The majority have more than £50 000 available, while almost a third have in excess of £100 000 available to invest in unquoted ventures.

These findings reinforce the work of Freear, Sohl and Wetzel (1994), who found that potential investors in the USA are not necessarily opposed to investing in entrepreneurial ventures, but would prefer to make investments on a smaller scale than active Angels. In dollar terms they found that over 75 per cent of all potential Angels, and over 60 per cent of interested potential Angels, would limit their investment in any one venture to less than $10 000. In contrast, almost half of the Business Angels who they surveyed would commit more than $24 000 to a single venture.

Our research also suggests that the investment activity of Virgin Angels is not generally curtailed by a lack of available funds: only 15 per cent of the group attribute their inactivity to this. Rather, we found that a difficulty in locating suitable business proposals was the principal reason (stated by almost two-thirds of the sample) for the inactivity of Virgin Angels. This reinforces that the problems of information transfer represent the biggest hindrance to the further expansion of the informal venture capital market.

There are other issues that restrict the investment activity of Virgin Angels. These include a lack of faith in the owner/manager of the venture (cited by 26

Table 9.1 Level of Funds Available for Informal Investment: Virgin Angels and Active Angels Compared

Size of available portfolio	< £50 000	£50 000–£100 000	£100 000–£200 000	£200 000–£500 000	£500 000–£1 million	> £1 million
Virgin Angels	38%	32%	19%	8%	3%	–
Active Angels*	24%	27%	19%	17%	4%	7%

* These figures refer only to the funds that active Angels have still available for investment; they exclude existing Angel investments.

per cent), a lack of reliable information (21 per cent), and a lack of experience in pricing equity stakes (18 per cent).

These findings partly reflect Mason and Harrison's (1993) research of British Angels, which found that 43 per cent of potential Angels considered the risks of informal direct investment to be too high, and that one-third of potential Angels felt that they lacked the investment appraisal skills necessary to make successful informal investments. In addition, a third of the potential investors who they studied were concerned about their ability to profitably liquidate informal investments.

Our study found that 86 per cent of Virgin Angels intend to make one or more Angel investments in the next five years. There are a number of factors that this group of potential investors feel would further encourage them to provide finance to unquoted businesses. Virgin Angels resemble each of the other active Angel types in that they believe a better knowledge of the founder/manager of a venture would improve their likelihood of making a deal. In all, over half of Virgin Angels believe that a better relationship with a prospective venture owner/manager would further encourage them to make this form of investment (see Figure 9.1). These findings reinforce the conclusions of Mason and Harrison (1993), who suggest that better knowledge of management and more trustworthy information would encourage Virgin Angels to make informal investments.

Virgin Angels are also concerned with how they would ultimately withdraw their investment from the venture and would like to see more clearly available exit routes, such as an unlisted stock market. Slightly more than a third of Virgin Angels would like to see better tax incentives to encourage this type of investment. In terms of specific government initiatives to encourage informal investment, this project found that over a third of Virgin Angels believe that

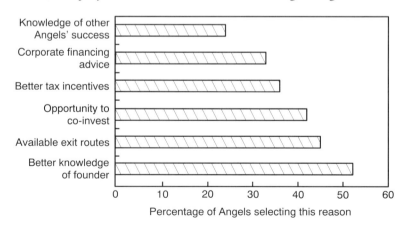

Figure 9.1 Factors that would Encourage Virgin Angels to Increase their Investment Activity

the Enterprise Investment Scheme (EIS) will be more likely to encourage informal investment activity than was the case with its predecessor the Business Expansion Scheme (BES). Further, the EIS has considerably greater support from Virgin Angels than from active Angel investors. The EIS allows investors who make investments in qualifying companies to invest up to £100 000 per annum, and receive 20 per cent tax back. In addition, there is no tax on capital gains made in the first five years of the investment. The biggest difference between the EIS and the BES is that investors are now allowed to take an active involvement in their investments, for example by sitting on the board. The fact that more Virgin Angels than active Angels are encouraged by this new initiative suggests that this government policy may be successful in increasing the number of individuals making informal investments.

Virgin Angels would also be encouraged to invest by the opportunity to co-invest with other more experienced investors (42 per cent). This desire for co-investment was also very evident among active Angels. The establishment of mechanisms such as the successful Oxford Trust, which brings large groups of potential investors together with entrepreneurs seeking finance, represents one way of increasing the level of co-investment among British Business Angels.

Almost a quarter of Virgin Angels would welcome the opportunity to gain a detailed knowledge of the successful investments of other Business Angels. Mechanisms that bring Angels of different types together would undoubtedly provide a forum for furnishing such information. In addition to these slightly informal mechanisms by which Virgin Angels could gain an understanding of how to make direct investments, over a third would like to be able to receive detailed, professional advice on making and structuring their Angel deals.

CHARACTERISTICS OF VIRGIN ANGELS

In Britain very little research has been done on the characteristics of Virgin Angels. Our research, which identified 143 Virgin Angels, found that they resemble active Angels in that they tend to be active, middle-aged and well-educated men. The study also suggests that while Virgin Angels are very well-off, they are significantly less wealthy than most active Angels. In addition they were found to be predominantly self-made, but were not as entrepreneurial as most of the active Angel types.

The Virgin Angels identified in this survey were almost exclusively male and their mean age was 46 years, which is slightly lower than the mean for active Angels (48 years). Most of the existing British and American research (Arum, 1989; Mason and Harrison, 1993; Wetzel and Freear, 1993) has found Business Angels to be very highly educated. The findings of this study suggest that Virgin Angels are also very well educated. Almost 60 per cent of this

Profile of Virgin Angels

- Average age   46 years
- Gender (percentage of males)   95%
- Education (percentage of university graduates)   57%
- Training (percentage with technical/professional training)   46%
- Sport (percentage that plays competitive sport)   83%

group have been to university, of which almost 20 per cent have postgraduate degrees, and half have had technical or professional training. This level of formal education is very similar to that found for active Angels, where half had been to university and almost half had technical or professional training. The study also discovered that Virgin Angels, like their active Angel counterparts, are very active individuals: over 80 per cent of the Virgin Angels who responded to the survey participated in some form of active competitive sport.

Financial and Business Backgrounds of Virgin Angels

- Net worth (excluding residence) > £200 000   59%
- Net worth (excluding residence) > £500 000   36%
- Annual income > £50 000   55%
- Number of substantial businesses founded   0.8

The survey found that Virgin Angels embraced people of very varied levels of wealth and income, although in general Virgin Angels are very well-off. After excluding the value of their principal residence, 59 per cent of them were worth more than £200 000 while over a third (36 per cent) were worth more than £500 000 and a quarter more than £1 million. In addition, the majority of these potential Angel investors continue to earn in excess of £50 000 a year.

Table 9.2 compares the wealth of Virgin Angels with that of active Business Angels who participated in the study. It is apparent that while Virgin Angels are indeed very well-off, they are significantly less wealthy than active Angels. In this regard the study disagrees with the conclusions of Mason and Harrison (1993) who suggested that Business Angels and potential Angels have similar financial backgrounds. We also found that there is no significant difference in the source of wealth between active and Virgin Angels. It is clear even from such an analysis of the net worth of Virgin Angels, that they have large financial resources at their disposal and that they are willing to invest in the informal venture capital market.

Table 9.2 The Net Worth of Virgin Angels and Active Angels Compared

Net worth (excluding principal residence)	< £50 000	£50 000– £100 000	£100 000– £200 000	£200 000– £500 000	£500 000– £1 million	> £1 million
Virgin Angels	12%	11%	18%	23%	11%	25%
Active Angels	3%	8%	16%	18%	20%	37%

A very important distinction between Virgin Angels and active Angels emerges when their entrepreneurial backgrounds are examined. On average Virgin Angels have started only 0.8 substantial new businesses (businesses employing more than five people or with a turnover of more than £1 million), with 57 per cent of them having never founded one. This represents a significantly lower level of entrepreneurship than that of active Business Angels, who have founded an average of 1.6 substantial businesses during their business careers. The fact that active Business Angels clearly have a greater degree of experience in founding new businesses, particularly in terms of practical hands-on knowledge of how to effectively finance these deals, may well contribute to their greater investment activity in the informal venture capital market.

INVESTMENT PREFERENCES OF VIRGIN ANGELS

This research suggests that Virgin Angels are seeking to make informal investments so as to create a job/income for themselves, and to earn greater returns than those earned on quoted shares (see Figure 9.2). In considering an informal investment Virgin Angels would focus on the personality of the venture founder/manager, their own experience in the industry sector, and the content and presentation of the business plan. This group of potential investors are also considerably more concerned with the geographic locations of ventures that they would consider backing than is the case for active Angel investors. Here we look at these investment preferences and compare them with those for active Business Angels.

The most commonly cited reason given by Virgin Angels for wanting to make this form of investment is their desire to create either a job or a regular income for themselves. Exactly half of them are looking to invest in unquoted ventures for this reason. This wish to use informal investments as a mechanism to create a job/income is more important for Virgin Angels than for active Angels. Virgin Angels also tend to be less concerned with pure financial returns than active Angels, and are less likely to make informal investments for fun or satisfaction than active Business Angels.

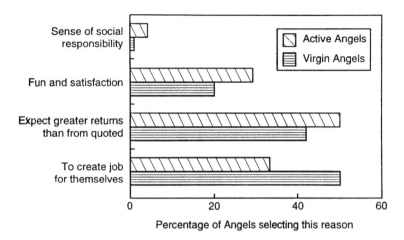

Figure 9.2   Reasons why Virgin Angels wish to make Informal Investments compared with why Active Angels do so

The criteria that Virgin Angels consider most important when assessing investment proposals are similar to those indicated by active Business Angels. The most important factor for Virgin Angels is their impression of the founder or manager of a venture. Almost 40 per cent of Virgin Angels pointed to this as being their principal investment criterion, which is considerably less than the nearly 60 per cent of active Angels who highlighted this factor. Virgin Angels appear to be willing to invest across most industry sectors, with only just over a quarter of them indicating that their own experience in, or understanding of, the industry sector in which the venture was located was the most important factor when assessing business proposals. This willingness to invest across industry sectors mirrors the investment activity and preferences of active Angel investors. It is interesting to note that more than a fifth of Virgin Angels consider the content and presentation of the business plans they receive to be the most important investment criteria. This is significantly higher than was the case for active Angels, and probably stems from the fact that Virgin Angels have less experience in making this form of investment than active Angels. As a result they may rely more on a formal, detailed investment proposal, rather than make an ad hoc judgement on the personality of the venture founder, when making their decision.

Virgin Angels are very much more concerned than active Angels with the proximity of a venture to their place of work (see Figure 9.3). Almost 60 per cent of Virgin Angels would not make an investment more than 100 miles from their place of work, which compares with only 40 per cent of active Angels who feel restricted to investing locally. Furthermore, over double the proportion of active Angels to Virgin Angels (44 per cent compared with 21

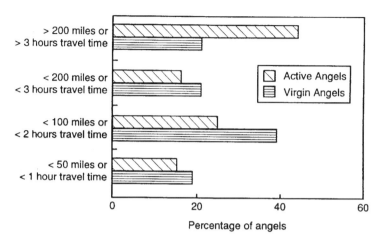

Figure 9.3 Maximum Distance from the Place of Work that Virgin Angels would Consider Making Informal Investments compared with Active Angels

per cent) would back an otherwise suitable venture that was located more than 200 miles away. This is an extremely important finding because it suggests that Virgin Angels, and not active Angels, share the concern with venture location that previous researchers (e.g. KPMG, 1992; Mason and Harrison, 1993, 1995) have attributed to active Business Angels.

Table 9.3 summarises the general deal preferences for Virgin Angels and compares them with those for active Business Angels. It is clear that the preferences of these two groups are very similar in terms of how they would like to see their deals structured, and their expectations for the performance of these deals. The majority of both groups favour co-investment while roughly a third of both groups seek majority stakes. Virgin Angels look for similar levels of returns and growth as active Angels and both would look to exit their ventures after about six years. This supports the findings of Freear, Sohl and Wetzel (1994) in America who found that Business Angels and interested potential Angels had similar preferences with regard to

Table 9.3 Deal Preferences and Expectations of Virgin Angels Compared with those of Active Angels

Expectation	Virgin Angels	Active Angels
Level of co-investment	51% favour co-investment	52% favour co-investment
Size of shareholding	39% prefer majority stakes	34% prefer majority stakes
Turnover of venture	£3 000 000 (5 years)	£2 600 000 (5 years)
Rate of annual growth	22%	22%
Rate of annual return	18%	19%
Timeframe for exit	6 years	6 years

co-investment and holding period. The most obvious difference between Virgin and active Angels is that, to date, Virgin Angels have been unwilling to take the plunge and actually make an informal investment.

SUMMARY FOR VIRGIN ANGELS

Virgin Angels are that group of inactive investors who have not yet made an investment in an unquoted venture. Existing American and British research suggests that there are many more Virgin Angels than active Angels. The key points to remember about Virgin Angels are:

- They are private individuals who are looking to provide finance to new or growing businesses, with a view to creating a job or a regular income for themselves, and to earn higher returns than those available on the stock market.
- They are not as wealthy as active Business Angels and have fewer funds available to invest, although they do still have considerable funds at their disposal.
- They do not cite this lack of funds as restricting their investment activity, but instead point to an absence of suitable investment proposals.
- Better knowledge of the founder/management team of prospective ventures, more clearly available exit routes, opportunities to co-invest with more experienced Angels, better tax incentives, and the availability of professional advice in structuring and monitoring investment deals would encourage Angels to make informal investments.
- They are more concerned with the geographic proximity of prospective investments than active Angels.

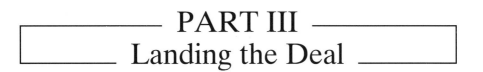

PART III
Landing the Deal

10

Increasing Angels' Investments

RESTRICTIONS ON INVESTMENT

Our research was concerned with examining the actual and potential level of investment activity of British Business Angels. There is a perception that the level of informal investment activity in Britain could be increased (e.g. KPMG, 1992; Mason and Harrison, 1993; Mason, Harrison and Allen, 1995; National Westminster Bank, 1993; van Osnabrugge, 1998). The locally focused Department of Trade and Industry (DTI) sponsored institutes, and the recently introduced Enterprise Investment Scheme (EIS) are examples of policy initiatives designed to promote increased informal investment activity. In an effort to discern whether or not the general level of investment activity could be increased this study was concerned with three related questions:

1. Do Business Angels have resources available for further investment?
2. What restricts the current investment activity of Business Angels?
3. Are there specific factors that could raise the level of informal investment?

This section seeks to determine the potential of the informal venture capital market and identifies specific ways by which this potential could be realised. The research was concerned both with examining ways by which the hindrances restricting active Angels could be overcome, and with increasing the investment activity of Angels who are already active investors.

Both active and inactive Angels have substantial funds available for further investment. Table 10.1 details the level of unallocated funds these two groups have available for investments in unquoted ventures. Even after investing an average of £265 000 almost half of active Angels have in excess of £100 000 available specifically for informal investments. National Westminster Bank (1993) estimated that Angels have an average of £165 000 available for informal investment. Mason and Harrison (1994a) found that Angels had an

Table 10.1 Level of Funds Available for Further Investment for Active and Inactive Angels

Size of the investment portfolio	< £50 000	£50 000– £100 000	£100 000– £200 000	£200 000– £500 000	£500 000– £1 million	£1 million– £5 million	> £5 million
Unallocated informal investment portfolio of active Angels (%)	24	27	19	17	4	7	–
Unallocated investment portfolio of inactive Angels (%)	36	29	20	8	4	2	–

average of £50 000 available for further investment. This study agrees with the National Westminster Bank estimates.

It is interesting to note that even after investing substantial funds active Angels still have more capital available for further informal investments than inactive Angels. Only a third of inactive Angels have more than £100 000 available for this form of investment. This finding challenges Mason and Harrison (1993), who suggest that the two groups have similar levels of funds available for Angel investment. The research of Freear, Sohl and Wetzel (1994) supports the findings of this project. They found that potential Angels are willing to invest a smaller percentage of their total portfolio, and look to make smaller individual investments than active Business Angels. While this research project would contend that these groups have significantly different levels of available funds, it is clear that both groups do have large amounts of funds available for Angel investments.

This study found that approximately 70 per cent of both active and inactive Angels anticipate increasing their level of investment activity in the next five years. In this regard the research reinforces the work of Mason and Harrison (1994a), who suggest that three-quarters of informal investors would like to make more investments. However, a number of factors restrict the investment activity of Business Angels, as outlined in Table 10.2 and explained in the chapters on the individual Angel types (Chapters 4–9). It is very interesting to note that the single biggest factor restricting the investment activity of Business Angels is not a lack of available funds, but rather a lack of suitable investment proposals. More than two-thirds of both active and inactive Angels cited this as the principal reason preventing them from making further investments. By way of contrast, only about a quarter of active Angels, and one-fifth of inactive Angels, felt restricted by a lack of available funds.

The problem of a shortage of suitable proposals was confirmed when 63 per cent of Business Angels stated that they would have made a greater number of informal investments during the past three years if they had had access to more suitable investment proposals. This finding on the problem of locating suitable proposals mirrors the research of Mason and Harrison (1993), who

Table 10.2 What Prevents or Restricts Active and Inactive Angels from Investing in Unquoted Ventures

Reasons*	Active Angels (%)	Inactive Angels (%)	Statistical significance level
Lack of suitable business proposals	70	67	Not significant
Lack of faith/trust in founder/manager	40	30	More for active Angels at 5%
Lack of reliable information	32	21	More for active Angels at 5%
Lack of available funds	27	19	More for active Angels at 10%
Lack of experience in pricing equity stakes	16	18	Not significant
Other	25	21	Not significant

* Respondents could indicate one or more.

suggest that 70 per cent of Business Angels would invest more if they could locate the right kind of investment opportunity. Clearly Business Angels have sufficient funds available to significantly increase their level of investment activity. The challenge for entrepreneurs, small businesses and policy makers is to find mechanisms to get the best investment proposals on to the desks of these Business Angels.

Two other related factors significantly restrict the investment activity of Business Angels. Forty per cent of active Angels are prevented from making further investments by a lack of faith in the founder/manager of the proposed venture. Mason and Harrison (1994b) and van Osnabrugge (1998) also found that problems with the entrepreneur or the management team were the biggest deal killer. Table 10.3 illustrates how developing the level of interactions between Angel and entrepreneur could help to address this concern. A significant number of Angels cite lack of reliable information flows as restricting their activity. Both of these factors stem from inefficiencies in information transfer in the informal venture capital market.

Table 10.3 highlights some of the factors that could increase the investment activity of Business Angels. This study found that better knowledge of/trust in the founder/manager, more clearly available exit routes, and improved tax conditions would be the factors most likely to increase British Business Angel investment activity. These findings support the findings of other British researchers (Hay and Abbott, 1993; Mason and Harrison, 1993; National Westminster Bank, 1993; van Osnabrugge, 1998) who identified the founder/management team, the business idea, tax incentives and exit routes as key

Table 10.3 Factors that would Encourage Active Angels and Inactive Angels to Invest in Unquoted Ventures

Factors*	Active Angels (%)	Inactive Angels (%)	Level of statistical significance
Better knowledge of/trust in founder/manager	63	54	More for active Angels at 10%
Better tax incentives	44	35	More for active Angels at 10%
Available exit routes, such as an unlisted stock market	44	45	Not significant
Opportunity to co-invest with experienced investors	38	41	Not significant
Knowledge of other Angels' successful investments	24	24	Not significant
Corporate financing advice on making/structuring investments	14	21	More for inactive Angels at 10%
Other	23	22	Not significant

* Respondents could indicate one or more.

Angel concerns. Our research also suggests that available corporate advice would be more likely to increase the investment activity of inactive Angels than active Angels.

SUMMARY

Both active and inactive Angels are keen to increase their level of investment activity and have the financial resources to do so; however, they have difficulty locating suitable investment proposals. In particular, Business Angels would like to obtain better information on the venture founders and identify more clearly available exit routes for them to recoup their investment. Better tax incentives would also help.

11
How to Raise Capital

The previous chapters in this book have looked at the different types of Angel investor available to the entrepreneur, categorised from our findings from a large-scale research project which examined nearly 500 Angels and profiled 467 different investment deals. In this chapter we provide entrepreneurs with a practical toolkit and set of action steps they can use to successfully target and locate particular Angel investors. We will look at the importance of the business plan, general sources of capital available to entrepreneurs, choosing the most appropriate source, locating potential investors, and the information preferences of investors. At the end of the chapter we will detail specific action steps that we feel entrepreneurs should take.

FROM THE OUTSET DEVELOPING A BUSINESS PLAN IS ESSENTIAL

It is vital that the entrepreneur prepares a business plan. This serves as a model for the business and forces the entrepreneur to adopt a managerial mindset. The process of developing such a plan should be iterative and consultative. By this we mean that the entrepreneur should draw on all available resources and contacts in preparing the plan and develop it in a stepwise manner which gradually refines and hones the document into a real vision for the business. While the final plan will certainly be used to attract investors, the process of developing the plan will be of enormous benefit to entrepreneurs. There is no single obvious model for drawing up a business plan, but we provide some guidelines in Chapter 12 for preparing this very important document.

THERE ARE TWO PRINCIPAL SOURCES OF CAPITAL AVAILABLE TO ENTREPRENEURS

At a very broad level there are two main categories of capital available to entrepreneurs. First of all there is the formal sector, which is made up of the stock market, venture capital companies, banks, government grants, and hybrids of these organisations. However, these organisations tend not to be interested in making the small-scale, high-risk investment that entrepreneurs require. Fortunately there is a second category of capital that caters for new and early stage businesses. This informal market, which is made up of about 50 000 private individuals and small company investors, currently provides approximately £2–4 billion per annum to unquoted businesses. These investors typically invest less than £250 000 in equity finance and often also bring practical business and entrepreneurial experience to the ventures they back. Typically these informal investors are referred to as Business Angels.

THERE ARE AT LEAST SIX DIFFERENT TYPES OF BUSINESS ANGEL

Most of the existing research on Business Angels, in both Britain and America, tends to treat Business Angels as a single homogeneous group of individual investors. Our study, which drew on a survey of nearly 500 active and potential Angels, found that a variety of very different types of investor fall under the umbrella term Business Angel. The research used cluster analysis to isolate four distinct types of active Angel investor: Entrepreneur Angels, Wealth Maximising Angels, Income Seeking Angels and Corporate Angels. Each of these have very different levels of investment activity, come from different financial and business backgrounds, invest for different reasons, and bring different value-added contributions to the ventures they back. The characteristics of these investors are summarised in Table 11.1 and are detailed in Chapters 4–7.

The key distinctions between the different types of active Angel investor can be seen in the matrix in Figure 11.1. This places the Angels into quadrants using financial and business background and level of investment activity as the two dimensions.

In addition to the Business Angels who are currently making investments in new and growing businesses, we also looked at interested potential Angels. There may be as many as ten times as many interested potential Angels as there are currently active Angels. We identified the Virgin Angel (see Chapter 9) and the Latent Angel (Chapter 8) as two examples of types of inactive Angel who could provide capital to the entrepreneur. Virgin Angels are wealthy, self-made individuals who have not previously made informal

Table 11.1 Summary of the Four Types of Active Angel Investor

Characteristics	Entrepreneur Angel	Wealth Maximising Angel	Income Seeking Angel	Corporate Angel
Total funds invested	£590 000	£131 000	£35 000	£540 000
No. of investments	3.4	2.1	1.5	3.0
Personal net worth	74% > £1 m	43% > £1 m	75% < £0.2 m	–
Number of businesses founded	4.0	1.3	0.4	–
Reason for investing	Returns/fun	Returns	Job/income	Returns/ SOSR*
Venture location	Unimportant	Unimportant	Some concern	Some concern

* SOSR is a "sense of social responsibility"

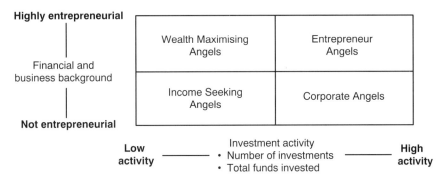

Figure 11.1 The Investment Activity and Characteristics of the Different Angel Types

investments, but are now interested in doing so. Latent Angels are individuals who want to invest again in entrepreneurial ventures, having been inactive for a number of years. For certain types of entrepreneur, investing with these types of Angel may be more attractive than investing with the other, more experienced Angel investors. The next section offers specific guidelines to entrepreneurs on the type of Angel investor that would be the most suitable investor for them.

CHOOSING THE MOST APPROPRIATE TYPE OF ANGEL

Entrepreneurs need to actively choose the most suitable Angel on the basis of their financial and managerial requirements. The matrix in Figure 11.2 should help you make these kinds of choices. The horizontal axis represents the level

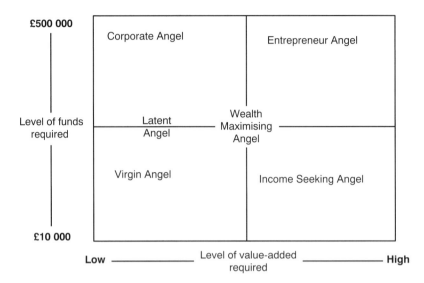

Figure 11.2   Entrepreneurs should Choose an Angel to Suit their Financial and Managerial Requirements

of value-added you are looking for. The Angels that offer the highest levels of value-added are Entrepreneur Angels and Income Seeking Angels.

Typically, Entrepreneur Angels have substantial business and/or entrepreneurial experience, which can be of great benefit to the ventures they back, particularly for inexperienced entrepreneurs. Income Seeking Angels tend to take full-time positions in the ventures they back and can draw on business experience, which can greatly help a new and growing venture. However, not all entrepreneurs want to have their investors meddling in the day-to-day operations of their ventures. For example, an experienced entrepreneur, with a top-class management team probably does not want the investors to play an active role in the investment. In this case, perhaps a Virgin or Latent Angel would be a more appropriate business partner. Angels should be targeted according to the type of role the entrepreneur would like the investor to play, as well as for the level of funding required.

BUSINESS ANGELS CAN BE LOCATED THROUGH A NUMBER OF SOURCES

The most common sources Business Angels use to locate investment opportunities are shown on the graph in Figure 11.3. It is clear that the bulk of opportunities are sourced through the personal and business networks of

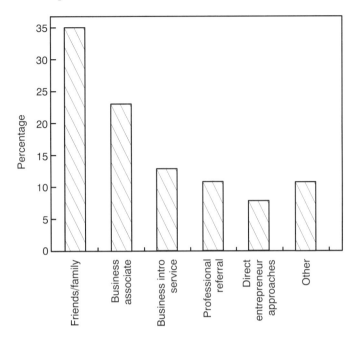

Figure 11.3 Sources of Information for Deals

Business Angels. Clearly it is important that entrepreneurs develop their own networks so that when the time comes to raise funds for their ventures they have a group of people and businesses that they can call on. This process is time-consuming, but the long-term benefit can be considerable.

There are other ways entrepreneurs can contact Business Angels. Two of the more common methods are selected press advertising and targeted mailing of local business people. However, both of these methods tend to be unfocused and can be a considerable drain on already scarce resources. In addition, we suggest taking legal advice before using either of these methods, since these areas are governed by the Financial Services Acts.

Another approach, which is now becoming more widely used, is to use advisers or intermediary organisations, such as business introduction services, to locate investors for the venture. Typically, they profile business ventures in monthly magazines bought on subscription. Subscribers pay an annual fee so they are very likely to be interested in making investments in new and growing businesses. Using these organisations is a cost-effective way of getting business proposals on to the desks of potential investors. But the help of business introduction services ends here, and the rest is up to the entrepreneur. Business introduction services are looked at in more detail in Chapter 14 where a number of such services are profiled.

TARGET ANGELS SELECTIVELY

It is very important for entrepreneurs to try to isolate Angels who may have an interest in the business field of the venture. We found that 80 per cent of the venture proposals Angels receive are of no interest to them. However, the entrepreneur that actually interests an Angel has a 25 per cent chance of receiving an offer of finance. Clearly, then, you need to think very clearly about the types of potential investors to whom your venture would be of interest. There are three things you can do to help find the right investor.

First, you should seek to establish an ongoing relationship with a prospective investor. The single most important question Angels ask when assessing proposals is whether or not they can trust the entrepreneur. Often it is difficult for the entrepreneur to gain that trust purely with a business plan and a number of follow-up meetings. If there is already a relationship based on trust and reliability, you need only to sell the business idea to the potential investor.

Second, as a starting point you should look to potential investors with a clear knowledge of, or interest in, the industry in which your venture is located. A substantial number of the Angels we surveyed were more comfortable making investments in industries they understood.

Third, we feel it is very important to understand that informal investment is a national rather than a regional phenomenon. For the 467 investments we examined the average distance of the venture from the investor's home was 97 miles. Furthermore, almost 50 per cent of the Angels were willing to back suitable ventures located more than 200 miles away. Consequently we would urge you not to confine your search to local Angels, but to look for suitable Angels regardless of their geographic proximity.

SPECIFIC ACTION STEPS

In conclusion, you should take the following specific action steps:

- prepare a plan
- decide on the most appropriate type of Angel for the venture
- develop a contact strategy
- go for it!

12
Creating a Convincing Business Plan

In this chapter we discuss a vital element of raising venture capital, regardless of the type of Angel you obtain funding from—a convincing business plan. A business plan is important for many reasons, but two stand out:

- it is a critical tool in your campaign to convince others to invest in your start-up venture
- it forces you to carefully and thoroughly consider the key issues facing your fledgling venture and hence convert your pipe dream into a reality.

A well-written business plan serves to demonstrate to your potential investors that you have a carefully considered, well thought-out business proposition. The following are all quotes from Business Angels we surveyed:

"Throughout the decision process I relied a lot on the business plan, my own investigations, and my impression of the entrepreneur. But the business plan foremost."

"The business plan has to be convincing; I have to believe the story and the implementation plans."

"The business plan has to be sound and I want to see evidence that the business idea is viable."

"I try to do as much research into a firm as I can and I usually start with the business plan, then the accounts, and then I talk to the people."

"I will only invest if the numbers in the business plan always come out right, no matter how they are analysed."

"The firm that I invested in didn't have a business plan but that was because it was already a few years old and running well. I ended putting one together before I invested."

"I don't like the way entrepreneurs present the cash flows as the most crucial part of the business plan, the core foundations (of the business) have to be realistic first."

"I like to see entrepreneurs who have gone to a lot of trouble to make up a good business plan, and placed lots of thought into it."

"It is imperative that the business plan is soundly written and contains realistic figures."

At the centre of an Angel's view of an entrepreneurial opportunity is the degree of risk associated with the project. What are the entrepreneur's chances for success or failure? The greater the risk of failure, the less interested most Angels will be, or they at least will want a higher rate of return in order to put up their hard earned pounds. The rate of return an Angel requires can be calculated by adding a risk factor, which varies from business to business, to the basic cost of capital for a FTSE (Financial Times Stock Exchange) "blue chip" firm. The basic cost of capital for big firms is based on the interest rate established by the Bank of England as the base plus a risk factor inherent in investing, even in the safest of firms. That is why government bonds have among the lowest returns in the marketplace: they are seen as being almost risk free—if the British government goes bankrupt we are all in great trouble. Governments tend to offer a small risk premium over the basic interest rate set up by the Bank of England. For a well-known, long-established, reputable firm traded on the Stock Exchange the rate required on top of the rate for bonds is small, perhaps 3 or 4 per cent. For a successful established firm it may have to pay a risk premium of 5, 6 or 7 per cent, depending on its record, previous borrowings and debt structure. For existing small firms, similar rates or slightly higher would be required, again depending on the existing debt and how impressed the lending institution or Angel is by the owner (see Figure 12.1).

For start-ups the risk premium would generally be even higher. Managing the perception of riskiness of the venture is an important early task. We believe that perception is less important than the hard-nosed realities of a new venture, and a well-presented business plan promotes a favourable first impression. A carelessly prepared or inadequate one has the opposite effect. Of course, the personal impression that an entrepreneur leaves is equally important to convincing an Angel that they are dealing with a sound business opportunity.

The business plan is the document that the Angel will have to take away to consider at their leisure, a document they may well show to other investors or advisers to help them in their decision making. It can act as your "foot in the door" to gaining the interest of an Angel.

This chapter is an important one for every entrepreneur because a sound business plan is an important key to bringing funding sources on board.

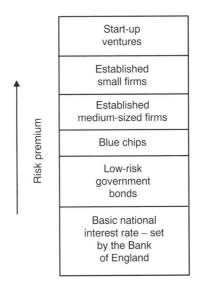

Figure 12.1   Risk Premium Diagram

Perhaps even more importantly, the discipline of thoroughly preparing a business plan helps to minimise the possibility of failure and substantially increases the likelihood of success.

Later in this chapter we discuss each of the key parts of a business plan.

PRESENTING THE BUSINESS PLAN

First impressions count for a lot, and the business plan is often the first and best opportunity an entrepreneur has of presenting a professional image. Therefore, care must be taken over the appearance of the business plan. Clearly Angels make their final investment decision based on the business merits of a proposal, but a well put-together plan can create a positive first impression, as the following quotes from Business Angels testify:

> "I always want to see a professional business plan. If there are any typing faults, I throw it away without considering it further."

> "The business plan must be well presented. It must be a well covered skeleton if it is going to attract my interest."

> "I like a serious business plan that is well thought out. If it's outlandish then that's an immediate turn off."

Our experience suggests that an entrepreneur with no business plan or one slapped together with a minimum of care will stand little chance of success. The old idea, "build a better mouse-trap and the world will beat a path to your door", simply rarely works any more—if it ever did! We have seen many "unbeatable" ideas fail, not because of any weakness in the original idea but because of poor marketing of the concept to investors. This is not an argument for appearance over substance or that a bad idea can succeed through slick presentation, but simply a recognition of basic investor psychology.

DOCUMENTS TO SUPPORT A BUSINESS PLAN

When presenting your business plan to an Angel we suggest that you also include:

- a cover letter (see Figure 12.2)
- a title page (see Figure 12.3)
- a table of contents (see Figure 12.4).

Given the importance of your venture's plan we recommend that you have the plan professionally prepared and bound. The binding can be done at low cost at any number of high street office products outlets. For a professional appearance you should ensure that, at least:

- Your business plan is prepared using a word processor and printed on a quality printer such as a laser.
- It is free of spelling and grammatical mistakes.
- It is neatly packaged and bound.
- It contains business language.
- The final version of your business plan is pre-tested by at least two people: one for language, grammar and general appearance; the second for the business merits of your plan—ask a person with considerable business experience to read through it.

The cover letter is your opportunity to tailor your proposal to the individual Angel you are approaching. The letter is best kept brief and to the point and written in clear and concise language. In most cases, if you write a several page cover letter a busy Angel will simply skip it. A sample cover letter to an Entrepreneur Angel is given in Figure 12.2. We have tailored it for an Entrepreneur Angel by suggesting the importance of the consulting role the Angel could have in ensuring the future success of this particular enterprise.

In the business plan itself we suggest that you tailor the amount and type of material you include to the type of Angel you are courting. For example, for a Corporate Angel you may wish to put a greater emphasis on the shorter-term

30 August 1997

Mr David Gunn
1234 Islip Road
Oxford
OX1 4JD

Dear Mr Gunn

Venture Capital

I enjoyed meeting you at the recent venture capital meeting. I feel that there is an unusually good match between your background and my new venture. My sense is that your years in the publishing industry and your previous small high-tech business experience would be of great benefit in helping this venture to become the success it has the promise to be.

As we discussed, I enclose a copy of the business plan for my firm, British Publishing Software. The key points discussed are an industry analysis of where we see the future of software in the UK publishing industry, a brief history of our management team, a sales forecast, and an operating and financial budget for the next three years. It represents a considerable amount of time and careful thought on the part of our management team.

Thank you for your kind consideration. I look forward to the opportunity to hear your further comments on this new venture proposal. I will give you a call later in the week to set up a meeting.

Yours sincerely

John Halford

Encs

Figure 12.2   Sample Covering Letter to an Entrepreneur Angel

sales forecast and cash flows to help them to see that they are considering a venture that is less risky than other new ventures. For an Income Seeking Angel you may focus on the opportunity for them to generate a position for themselves in the not too distant future as the venture grows.

The key starting point is to understand yourself and your venture and then use the Angel Matching Matrix to identify the type of Angel which best fits your needs. With the best type of Angel for your venture firmly in mind you are in a better position to develop a persuasive business plan using the model presented in this chapter as your basic framework.

Business Plan
British Publishing Software
Elstree House
Elstree Way
Borehamwood, Herts
(0181) 316 283

John Halford, Managing Director

30 August 1997

The content of this business plan is confidential and is the property of British Publishing Software. Its use is limited to those authorised by the Managing Director of British Publishing Software. Any reproduction or divulgence of the contents of this business plan without the written consent of British Publishing Software is prohibited

---

Figure 12.3 Sample Title Page for a Business Plan

Cover Letter
Title Page
Table of Contents

Executive Summary
   Business Concept
   Operating Plan Summary
   Marketing Plan Summary
   Financial Plan Summary

Business Description
   Business History
   Management/Key People
   Products/Services

Operating Plan
   Operating Procedures
   Facilities and Layout
   Purchasing and Distribution
   Inventory Management
   Customer Service

Industry Analysis
   Industry Five Forces Framework
   Industry Competition
   Competitive Threats
   The Industry's Future and Sales Projections

Market Analysis
   Target Market
   Market Competition
   Sales Forecast

Financial Plan
   Historical Analysis
   Budget Projections

Figure 12.4 Sample Table of Contents for a Business Plan

THE COMPONENT PARTS OF THE BUSINESS PLAN

Executive Summary

The executive summary is a brief, one or two page summary of your proposal. Undoubtedly, the single most important section of your business plan is the executive summary. If you require additional help beyond that given in this chapter, we recommend you contact your local Business Link office[1] for help and/or consult any of the number of good books on the market that focus exclusively on preparing business plans (e.g. Abrams, 1993; Thomas and Fredenberger, 1995).

You need to present a clear, concise and convincing summary of your business plan to encourage potential investors to read through the rest of it. In our experience, most Angels will turn first to the executive summary. If you do not capture their interest and attention here, they will toss your proposal in the "no further action required" pile. Whether they continue reading beyond the summary depends on the content and the quality of your writing. In this section we will outline what is typically included in an executive summary, suggest two types of executive summaries and explain those rare occasions when an executive summary should not be included.

Contents of an Executive Summary

The executive summary is a brief synopsis of the key issues in the business plan. What you are trying to convey in your summary is that:

- your basic business concept makes sense
- you have done a thorough job of analysing the industry
- a clear target market segment exists
- you have a clear competitive advantage
- the management is capable.

In most cases you would include a concise description of:

- the venture's basic business
- how and where the business will be conducted
- the target market or the venture's products/services and the sales potential in the target market
- what sustainable competitive advantage the venture brings to the market
- the financial resources needed to implement the plan.

Two Types of Executive Summary[2]

Depending on the type of Angel you are trying to reach and your writing skills you can approach the summary in one of two ways: the synopsis summary or the narrative summary.

The *synopsis summary* is the easier of the two. It presents in brief the key points of each section of the full business plan. Although this approach is relatively straightforward to prepare, it can come across as rather dry. It is, however, probably the more business-like of the two styles and would probably be the best to use with Corporate, Latent and Virgin Angels.

The *narrative summary* tells a story. The chief advantage of this approach is that it can draw your reader into the drama of the story and create a degree of involvement that the synopsis summary cannot. However, it takes a good writer to do this successfully. A narrative summary is perhaps most useful for businesses that are doing something out of the ordinary—that is, they are breaking new ground or have interesting or impressive histories.

According to Abrams (1993), a narrative summary has fewer sections than the synopsis summary. The focus is on the central business concept and its unique features and less attention is given to the day-to-day details. A narrative summary often serves to set the scene, providing the evolution of the industry which has led to the unique opportunity presented in the business plan.

Suggestions for Preparing an Executive Summary[3]

Follow these points when preparing an executive summary:

- Write it last. This works best because a good executive summary is a concise and logical summary of your plan—this cannot be done until you have fully developed the entire vision of your venture.
- Keep the main message in mind. The thrust of the executive summary is why and how the new venture will succeed—don't wander too far from that.
- More risk needs more proof. A new venture, almost by definition, is more risky than an established firm, hence a business plan for a new venture must make a stronger case than for one for an existing business.
- Don't get carried away. Although you are trying to convince someone to invest significant funds in your venture, avoid the temptation to make exaggerated claims. Angels are generally sharp individuals who quickly see through overstatements.

- Keep it short. Abrams (1993) suggests that a busy Angel should be able to read the summary in five minutes, which means that it should be at most three pages. A one-page executive summary is fine.

The Business Description

As the name suggests, this part of the business plan outlines the basic nature and purpose of the business. A business description explains the answers to key questions that are naturally on the mind of an Angel, for example:

- What exactly is the business of the venture?
- What product or service does the venture plan to sell?
- Who is the target market for the venture?
- What key events in its history has brought the venture to where it is in its life cycle?
- Who is the management team?
- What is its competitive advantage(s)?

Suggestions for Preparing the Business Description

We suggest you do the following for a business description:

- Draft it first. DeThomas and Fredenberger (1995) suggest that you prepare a draft of this section of your business plan first. They argue that doing so provides an indication of your understanding of the business and the adequacy of your planning effort.
- Write it last. DeThomas and Fredenberger suggest that this be one of the last sections you actually write. The idea is that it provides a synopsis of the entire business plan, hence it cannot be finished until the other sections are fully outlined.

Business History

An Angel often likes to understand the background of a business and how it got to where it is today. You are telling a story and you should try to make it interesting. In our experience, British Angels are even more interested in the history of the firm than are Angels in the USA.

Key points you may cover in the business history are:

- The firm's founding and founder(s).
- The form of ownership and any major changes that have occurred along the way.

- Any major achievements, such as big sales and significant turns.
- A brief description of any major crisis the firm has endured and how the management guided the firm through it.

Management/Key People

This is an opportunity to provide a thumbnail profile of each of the key players who will lead the business forward. You may possibly provide CVs for each of the top people. Here you want to demonstrate that qualifications and previous work experience has amply prepared them to take on the task ahead of them. Along with their backgrounds it is often helpful to provide a short description of their position and their primary duties. Most Angels would agree that a new venture's chances for success are only as good as the quality of the staff, especially the management.

Product/Services

Along with excellent people a new venture must have the "right" product or service to meet the needs of the target market. In this section you should present your product or service, together with the reasons you will put to your prospective clients/customers to persuade them to purchase it.

Operating Plan

Operations are the day-to-day running of the firm and how you are going to consistently deliver value to your customers. In larger companies the job of operations is often separated out from that of strategy and the biggest responsibility of executive management is strategy. In smaller firms the management team has to deliver on both operations and strategy. You tend to need an operating plan when the process you will be using is highly technical, new and unusual or in the case where operations are central to what you will be bringing to the marketplace.

Operating Procedures

Here the idea is to outline the operating process. The length of this section will depend on how technical, complicated and unusual operations are. You may not need this section in your business plan at all. Some Angels may only skim this section; others, who may know your industry, may spend a considerable time studying this section. Be careful how much detail you provide if you have a new approach—would you be concerned if your competitors were to see your plan?

If you have a revolutionary new approach, a key issue will be your ability to trade-off costs of your process with the value-added it brings to the market. Referring to a pilot site that has demonstrated the practicality of your figures would be helpful. Experience suggests that, all too often, initial actual production costs are higher than expected with new processes as teething problems surface. Not only is this true for new processes, it can also be true when you significantly increase the scale of your operations. What new staff will be necessary? Will an additional layer of management be required? What do you foresee as the "glitches" that will inevitably arise?

Facilities and Layout

Where your facilities will be and what they will look like are key questions in this section. Have you already lined up the facilities, or is this an outstanding item? How much room for growth have you allowed for—too little and your competition may steal a march on you; too much and you may be endangering your operation with too much overhead too early? It may be useful to provide a plan of your proposed facilities; it may even be worth building a model as a sales aid in seeking financing.

Purchasing and Distribution

This section may or may not be included, based on the relative importance of these activities in your firm. If your volumes are expected to be substantial in the first few years, answering the following questions may be helpful:

- Which purchases are critical to the firm's operations and why?
- Are key items available from a limited number of suppliers, or are they more widely available?
- What event triggers a purchase, or which person makes the decision to purchase key items?
- What vendors will you/are you using and how did you choose them?
- How reliable are these suppliers in terms of product availability, meeting lead times, service and quality assurance?
- What percentage of your firm's operating costs do the purchase components represent?
- What record-keeping system is used to track purchase orders?
- What aspect, if any, of the purchasing function is unique or provides a competitive advantage?

- What methods are used to ensure that suppliers are paid promptly and cash discounts are taken when available?

Inventory Management

As with the purchasing and distribution section the inventory management is optional, depending on the relative importance of these activities in your firm.

Three key elements required for an effective inventory management system are:

- A sound sales forecast, which leads the production schedule.
- Well thought out policies concerning which items are carried at what level, at what point inventory is reordered, and the safety stock carried. These elements are a carefully chosen balance between great customer service and costs of carrying the inventory.
- An information system that provides timely and reliable inventory data to management.

Customer Service

Now more than ever customer service is seen as a key component for winning business over your competition and, perhaps more importantly, for retaining customers. The days of shoddy service and treating customers poorly is long over in the UK. In many industries the ability to capture the flow-on revenues after initial purchase are more important than the purchase price. A historical example is that of Gillette, which had the idea of giving away their razors in order to help commit men to buying their blades for years.

One way of looking at this is to calculate the lifetime revenue stream of a customer. What, for example, is the value of a brake job to a garage? A hundred pounds or so, on the face of it. But if the customer is treated well and not taken advantage of, she will come back to you time and time again. If when she first comes to you, she is 20 years old, that could potentially represent well over £30 000 of car repairs in her lifetime. Treat her badly so that she goes elsewhere and you could be watching the equivalent of a new Rover for yourself walk out the door.

Industry Analysis

As much as we would like to, no company operates in a vacuum. Every new venture has to face the tough reality that it has competitors. The forces that impact your industry as a whole will also affect your business. An insightful industry analysis often increases your own understanding of the critical success factors that dominate an industry and demonstrates to Angels that you understand the important issues in your external business environment.

For the vast majority of new ventures it is fairly easy to say which industry you are in. An industry is generally defined as all firms supplying a similar product/service, other businesses closely related to that product/service, and supply and distribution systems supporting such firms (Porter, 1980). For example, the personal computer industry includes firms making PCs, suppliers who provide the component parts to manufacturers, and retail distribution outlets.

For some high-tech start-ups, deciding what industry you are in is not an easy question to answer. For example, for children's books on CD-ROM a case could be made for being in the multimedia industry or the children's publishing industry or the software industry. In these more grey areas we suggest that you focus on your most direct competitors, though be aware that in these emerging industries, new and unexpected competitors can sometimes quickly arise.[4]

Doing an Industry Analysis

The most useful tool we have found for performing an industry analysis is Michael Porter's (1980) Five Forces framework (see Figure 12.5).[5]

Threat of substitutes   With a new venture there is often a new approach or idea that the world or at least the UK has not seen before. Innovations, which are the life blood for many small ventures, often spring from the fertile minds and experiences of the entrepreneur or from importing ideas from overseas. Regardless of the source, all firms, even start-ups with exciting new innovations, are competing with industries producing substitute products or services. So even though Coke and Pepsi are bitter competitors they are not the only game in town—they also compete with other fizzy drinks, beer and even water. What this means for you is that you should consider two key questions in this section of your industry analysis:

- Why should potential customers leave their existing supplier to use your offering?
- What will keep them with you when they consider substitutes?

Bargaining power of suppliers   Suppliers can exert negotiating power over firms in an industry by threatening to raise prices or by reducing the quality of the goods. Powerful suppliers can squeeze profitability out of an

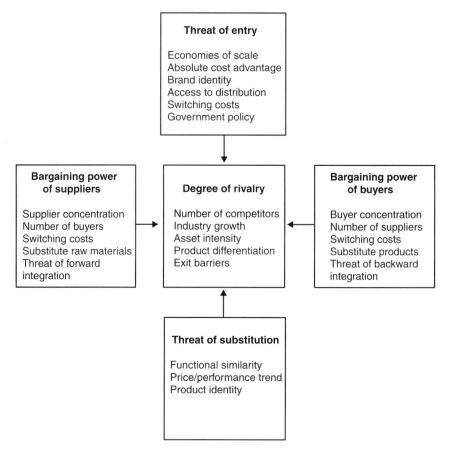

Figure 12.5   The Five Forces Industry Analysis Tool
Source: Porter, 1980

industry. Generally this is an issue relevant to firms that use a great deal of a supplier's product or where the supplier's product is in very great demand.

For most small firms this is only a problem when the supplier's product has few or no substitutes and the supplier is willing to squeeze the entrepreneur. Occasionally you may see this happening with franchises that are forced to buy a product from the franchiser; over time the franchiser may force them to take a certain amount of product or buy exclusively from them. The only time when we really need to worry about this section is when there is potential that your supplier could "hold a barrel over you".

Potential new entrants   The concern with this part of the five forces model concerns the potential that a new firm will enter the part of the in-

industry you compete in to dramatically change the nature of structure of competition—to your detriment. The concerns with new entrants are that they often bring new capacity, the desire to gain market share and often, substantial resources. In other words, they may substantially change the market you compete in, hence your backers are concerned that their investment may be threatened. What you wish to accomplish in this section is to demonstrate your understanding of the industry dynamics and how your approach will allow you to compete and prosper.

A key concept that helps in analysing the threat of new entrants is that of barriers to entry. Barriers to entry are simply the things that get in the way of new firms entering an industry. For small ventures they are the new entrants and so you can turn Porter's ideas on their head and in your business plan show how you can successfully get over the barriers to entry in the industry you are hoping to enter. Porter outlines six major sources of barriers to entry:

1. *Economies of scale.* These are the decline in unit costs of product as the volume per period increases—in other words, the more you make the cheaper it gets. Obviously economies favour larger firms over smaller firms, but there are some limits to how big an advantage economies of scales are in the late 1990s. Flexible manufacturing and mass customisation[6] have reduced the impact. In some industries economies of scale are still relevant, for example computer chip making and most forms of steel manufacturing, though mini-mills have even brought economies of scale in steel making into doubt.

2. *Product differentiation.* This has to do with the strengths of brands and the customer loyalty associated with brands (see Aaker, 1994, 1996; Chernatony and McDonald, 1992). Brands are built over time through advertising, customer service, developing relationships and longevity as a brand. It is harder to enter a market where brands mean a great deal, for example, Pepsi and Coke. A small firm with an innovative idea can carve out a niche for themselves in their market as long as they have a plan to enable them to show their advantage to leap over brand strength of their entrenched competitors.

3. *Capital requirements.* Some industries require a considerable amount of capital to establish themselves, for example to do expensive research and development or build a large plant. If you wish to start up a new semi-conductor plant it requires an enormous amount of money; starting up a new video shop could be done for considerably less!

4. *Switching costs.* For some customers the costs of switching from one competitor's product to another, is high. For example, when considering moving from one word processor to another the biggest single cost item would most likely be the retraining costs for staff, rather than the cost of

purchasing the software. For this reason, Word from Microsoft stands a very strong chance of maintaining its dominant market share. For a small venture, where there are switching costs, how do you address them in such a way that customers are willing to switch to your product?

5. *Access to distribution channels.* In some industries gaining access to the channels of distribution is a difficult business. Often small firms find it a considerable challenge to obtain shelf space in supermarkets, especially with the big players like Sainsbury's or Tesco. How will your new venture break into existing channels of distribution, or perhaps create new ones?[7]

6. *Government policy.* As small businesses know all too well at times, government can make it difficult to enter an area of activity. At the extreme are monopolies or quasi-monopolies, such as water or telephone service supply. For most industries there are thankfully few barriers put up by government except in terms of the basic requirements for reporting and paperwork.

Bargaining power of buyers   The issue for small business here is a simple one: are you too dependent on one or two customers? If they took their business away, would you go belly up? If a firm depends too much on one customer they are vulnerable—the buyer can, for example, too strongly bargain with the supplier (you) for discounts or equivalents. If you have traditionally depended on one or a few customers the question Angels would like to see discussed is what you will do to reduce that dependence.

Competitive rivalry   This refers to the intensity of rivalry among existing competitors. In some industries there may be collusion among the bigger players as they seek to divide up the market among themselves. For small businesses the issue is more at the local level and the degree of competition that you face in your area. In developing your business plan the focus here would be on demonstrating your knowledge of the competition and showing that you have sufficient understanding of how to successfully compete against them.

Industry Life Cycle Tool

Another helpful tool is the industry life cycle tool (see Table 12.1). You don't necessarily have to use both the five forces and the industry life cycle tool, but take a look at both and use your judgement as to their value in terms of developing your own understanding as well as using them to demonstrate your understanding to potential Angel investors.

Table 12.1 Industry Life Cycle Tool

Characteristic	Stage of Industry Life Cycle			
	Introduction	Growth	Maturity	Decline
Growth rate	High	Very high	Plateaued	Declining
Competition	Low	Very strong	Entrenched	Decreasing
Market leaders/ standards	None	Emerging	Fixed— dominant players	Contracting
Marketing goals	Exposure and credibility, often missionary	Differentiate from the competition	Industry leadership	Survival or dominating
Market share strategy	Gain foothold	Build market share	Maintain share	Cannibalise weakened competitors
Product range	Limited	Expanding	Broad	Reduced
Customer loyalty	None	Strengthening	Strong	Weakening

Source: Adapted from Abrams (1993) and Kotler and Turner (1995).

The four stages of the Industry Life Cycle

Introduction or emerging industries   These are ones where many new ventures are the norm. Smaller companies are often better at responding rapidly to the high degree of change that is often the mainstay of these new industries. Bigger firms often have not yet recognised the potential these industries represent or have chosen to sit on the sidelines until industry sales revenues are sufficient to justify their getting involved. These are new industries where the industry structure is yet to be established—they are often an excellent site for new ventures. Often a significant amount of time is spent by industry pioneers doing missionary work, helping customers new to the industry to understand the way products/services can meet previously unmet and/or understood needs.

  The concern many Angels have with new ventures in this stage of the industry life cycle is the high degree of risk they face. Risk is on two primary fronts: (1) that the industry won't take off, and (2) that it will take off, but that a giant firm will come in and dominate.

Growth industries   These enjoy rapid growth as customers begin to recognise the need for the product/service. These are new industries where the industry structure is beginning to be established, often a very good place for new ventures.

As growth markets begin to mature, competition becomes more intense as the growing market opportunities draw attention, from larger firms and often from other small new ventures started up by former employees who wish to cash in by forming their own ventures. In this stage the industry is still relatively unstructured as an industry standard is yet to emerge.

In high-tech industries this is often the time when one firm's offering becomes the industry standard—they are the clear winners and their revenues and profits often are considerably higher than those of their nearest rivals. In this type of high-tech environment there is often a fallout of smaller firms with a dominant winner and two or three other reasonably successful competitors.[8]

Mature industries These have arrived—the industry structure is relatively well established with competitors understanding each other's strengths, weaknesses and market position. The strong revenue increases of the growth stage are largely gone. Growth can cover a multitude of sins; during the mature stage those mistakes can "come home to roost". During this time customers tend to be brand loyal, for many products the decision to purchase has become a relatively standardised decision. During this period it is more difficult for new firms to break into the industry and to manage it they generally need a breakthrough that will put the firm ahead of the entrenched competition.

Declining industries These are on their way out—competition may be intense for diminishing revenues, with profit margins under great pressure. Typically customers are turning to other solutions to meet their needs. For example, the typewriter industry declined substantially as customers turned first to word processors and later to personal computers. But it is possible to compete profitably in declining industries, especially for small businesses staffed by managers who have long experience in the industry. You need to find a niche where there is less competition yet still a sufficient customer basis to support your firm. For example, we know of a manager in a company that serves Wang word processors; Wang was highly successful in the 70s and early 80s, but ran into some difficult times and eventually filed for bankruptcy. However, many law firms still use their old Wang equipment rather than spend the money to upgrade their secretaries to PCs. Clearly this is a declining market, but the service skills are still valuable to these law firms and there is money to be made.

To convince an Angel to invest in a new venture in a declining industry will take considerable effort. We suggest that you focus on your management team's experience, your intimate knowledge of the industry, the reduced degree of effective competition in the industry and your future growth plans. Fortunately for small businesses most large firms tend to ignore declining markets in favour of more "sexy" growth markets so that you may be on to a good opportunity.[9]

Market Analysis

The market analysis and sales forecast are the necessary companions to the industry analysis, which tends to be a more general and broad level of analysis. On the other hand, the market analysis and sales forecast represent more of the nitty gritty of the business plan. Here the grand vision you have painted in the industry analysis meets the short strokes and the reader begins to see the specifics of how your venture will, hopefully, perform. The industry analysis must suggest a strategic opportunity and its market must have a profitable niche. The sales analysis converts market potential into hard number targets, which are the driving force behind the activities of the firm.

Target Market

One of the first steps in developing your market analysis is to consider how your market might be segmented. In any industry there exists a number of ways of segmenting or cutting up your potential market. For examples see Table 12.2. Developing the appropriate segmentation base is not as easy as adopting the existing base your industry currently uses. You might well do so in the end, but you give up a potential competitive advantage if you do not build into your business plan time to reconsider how your industry segments its markets. A new approach to segmentation can be as potentially powerful as a new technology.

Table 12.2 Potential Bases of Segmentation for Consumer Markets

Usage	Potential segmentation bases			
	Demographic	Loyalty	Social	Psychographic
Frequency of use (heavy, medium, light)	Age	Price switchers	Income	Lifestyle
Brand loyalty	Gender	Passively loyal	Occupation	Interests
Product or service price level	Family life cycle	Fence sitters	Education	Opinions
Usage occasion	Race	Committed	Social class	Values

Source: Adapted from Kotler and Turner (1995), Aaker (1996) and DeThomas and Fredenberger (1995).

Target marketing is a simple, yet powerful idea—out of all the potential segments you could go after, which one(s) will you target as your primary focus? For many entrepreneurs it is tempting to go after every segment—it moves, sell it! The problem with this approach is that no firm, even an IBM or Unilever, has the resources to do this. It is wiser for a start-up to focus its precious resources on a small number of segments. The questions your potential Angel investors will want answered in your business plan are:

- What target markets have you chosen?
- What is the logic behind your choice?
- What compelling reasons are you offering your potential customers to buy from you?

In other words, what is your unique selling proposition (USP)?

Market Competition

In your industry analysis section you will have discussed competition in general. In this section you need to focus on your key three or four competitors. The key points that should be covered in the competitor assessment include:

- their unique selling proposition
- product/service differentiation
- pricing strategy
- target segments
- key management personnel
- financial strengths
- product/service quality.

Sales Forecast

The sales forecast is an estimate of expected sales volume for a specific future time period, typically in years. DeThomas and Fredenberger (1995) suggest that the sales forecast is the single most critical piece of information in the business plan. This is because:

- sales volumes are the most obvious indicator of future commercial success of the new venture, hence the sales forecast and its underlying assumptions will often be put under the magnifying glass by Angels
- sales potential is an important criteria for judging the value of a new venture—if the target market cannot produce a profitable level of sales you are in trouble from the start. A helpful approach is asking questions such

as: what percentage of the target market do we need to win in order to reach our sales forecast? If it is 50 per cent of the target market in the first three years, you should question your sales forecast
- the sales forecast acts as a foundation for other parts of the business plan. For example, it is the basis for the financial plan for estimating asset requirements and cash flow.

Sales forecasting is a fine art and one that is difficult at the best of times. There are various approaches that an existing firm can take, such as previous period plus growth factor, or previous period with a cyclical or seasonal movement. With a start-up it is more difficult—you have little firm history to guide you. Here, your industry experience will often come into play as you draw analogies to your experience in other firms.

The one-year forecast is expected to be reasonably accurate, though with a new start-up this may be also a bit difficult to do. Two and three year forecasts are useful from a viewpoint of showing how you will be able to provide a return to your Angel. Five years and longer are not very useful and are usually taken with a large dose of salt. Five years for any firm these days, especially for a start-up, is an eternity away and the world you compete in will undoubtedly change considerably during that time. According to research in North America (Cooper, 1993), new products[10] account for a staggering 40 per cent of company sales, on average. The research also suggests that the figure has been going up dramatically: 33 per cent in the years 1976 to 1981; 40 per cent from 1981 to 1986; and 42 per cent between 1985 and 1990. Difficult, yes, but nevertheless an important part of your business plan as it provides a base for the financial and operating plans.

Product Life Cycles

Product life cycles are very similar to the industry life cycle, however, they are much shorter and there are many products that run through their life cycle long before the industry life cycle is finished. For most industries product life cycles have shortened in the last decade—for example, the product life in the auto industry has gone from eight years at Ford to less than four years. In some high-tech industries continual improvements in the price performance of underlying chip technology,[11] and hyper competitive markets[12] drive product life cycles to be, for some products such as laptops, a year or less.

Adoption of Innovations—Why Some New Products Succeed and Others Fail

For a new venture with a new product/service which has not yet established a place for itself the theory of the adoption of innovations (see Rogers, 1995) can be a helpful way of understanding and explaining how you think your sales will grow. At the centre of encouraging customers to adopt an innovation is our human concern for reducing the risk of exchanging our old behaviour for new. The theory of adoption of new innovations or new ideas, whether they be a product, service or idea suggests that five key characteristics of innovation have a strong impact on how fast they are adopted by your target market. The characteristics are outlined below.

1. Relative advantage This is the degree to which an innovation is perceived as being better than the idea it supersedes. Most people, with the exception of innovators, are inherently conservative, and it takes a considerable reward to get them to change their behaviour. This is one reason why advertisements for competitors to BT feature such large discounts. Without considerable savings, why should consumers bother to contact another provider, have to pay a second bill and learn a new way of dialling long distance? BT's competitors have spent considerable effort to make it as easy as possible to use their services, but it still takes a considerable discount to attract people away from the comfortable old way to phone long distance.

A key difference here may be found between consumer and industrial marketing. Consumer markets are more apt to have what marketing theory calls low involvement goods—that is, goods that are frequent purchases, low in value and where the consumer gives little thought to the purchase. Industrial markets are more apt to involve high involvement goods—that is, goods or services where the product is infrequently purchased, higher in value and where the buying centre (more than one person involved in the purchase) gives considerable professional thought to the purchase. For low involvement goods the relative advantage has to be high in order to break through the little concern the consumer has for the purchase. For high involvement goods the relative advantage does not have to be as high. For example, if your firm offers a new tooling machine that is 15 per cent more productive than your competitors', many firms would consider talking to you. However, a 15 per cent savings on phone bills is insufficient to encourage the average British consumer to leave BT. Some consumer products can also be higher involvement, for example, a home, a car or an electronic good.

2. Compatibility This is the degree to which an innovation is perceived as consistent with the existing values, past experiences, and needs of potential adopters. This characteristic helps us understand why, for example, it is difficult for Lotus to get users to switch to their AmiPro word processor from Word or Word Perfect. The price of the AmiPro software is less of an issue than the time needed to learn how to use it. Most users have invested a number of hours to learning Word or Word Perfect and are loath to invest more time to learn a new programme unless the relative advantages are very large.

An example of an innovative product that has enjoyed considerable success is cellular phones. One reason that they have been widely adopted is that cellular phones are very compatible with customers' previous ways of making phone calls, i.e. land lines. The way of dialling and receiving calls is identical.

3. Complexity This is the degree to which an innovation is perceived as relatively difficult to understand and use. This third characteristic helps to understand why artificial intelligence products are not widely used today. Artificial intelligence is a complex idea that is not easy to grasp. On the other hand, voice mail has enjoyed considerable market penetration because it is easy for most people to understand.

4. Trialability This is the degree to which an innovation can be experimented with on a limited basis. The idea here is that the more you can reduce the risk to the customer of trying your innovation the more they will be willing to give it a try. This is one reason that we occasionally receive a small size bottle of shampoo or other consumer product through the letterbox. By reducing the risk to virtually nothing the consumer is much more likely to try out the product. The hope is that a significant number of tryers will then appreciate the experienced benefits enough to purchase the product.

In the high-tech arena, many software products are now available on the Internet for free for a 30 days trial, to encourage consumers to use the product at no charge. At the end of the thirty days the software will no longer work and the consumer has to contact the manufacturer's Web site to obtain a fully functional copy of the software for the retail price. It costs money to provide this trial, but if you are convinced that your product is so good that once consumers have used it for 30 days they will not want to live without it, it may be worth the risk.

5. Observability The easier it is for a consumer to observe the innovation in use the more likely they are to adopt it. By observing the product or service, the customer can see for themselves how easy the product is to use, hence reducing the risk in their minds of the innovation not working for them. This is why many firms set up booths at trade shows where they can demonstrate their products to key customers and distribution channels, and why many industrial sales include expensive visits to existing customers who are successfully using the product.

Financial Plan

The following quotes show how important prospective Business Angels consider financial plans.

> "Financial projections and other financial aspects of the firm, a detailed and well thought-out business plan, and an entrepreneur who has deeply thought through the business are all things which need to be present to be worthy of my further consideration of an investment."

> "The financial numbers and the reality behind the numbers should always be shown in the business plan. I always expect the cash flows to be done and well thought out."

Based on the marketing and sales plan the financial plan is an area of special interest to an Angel as it details how the Angel will recoup their investment and make a very healthy return. Entrepreneurs should not be embarrassed to realise that an excellent return is central to why an Angel invested. Certainly, as our research has pointed out earlier, being involved in an active business and fun are part of the reasons Angels invest, but a number are clearly obtaining a return far better than they would get from merely leaving money in a bank account or investing in the stock market. Key questions to answer in the financial plan include:

● What amount of financing is required to make the plans reasonable?
● When and in what flows will the financing be needed?
● Who will provide the financing?
● What will the project (pro forma) financial statements look like in a year?

To prepare the financial plan you can turn to several sources. The sales forecast provides the data to develop the cash flow statement and pro forma financial statements. The marketing budget provides estimates of product revenues and marketing expenditures, and the operating budget provides data on asset requirements and production schedule. Finally, industry sources can provide financial ratios typical for firms you are competing against.

Financial Goals

A key part of the financial plan is a set of financial goals—these are the benchmark measures used to measure the progress a firm is making. Without financial success a firm cannot remain viable.

Cash flows must be sufficient to ensure that you:

● meet monthly and annual expenses

- service debt obligations (this is of special interest to an Angel)
- replace assets as they become obsolete or wear out
- earn an adequate rate of return for the owner and Angel.

Some common measures you should include are:

- percentage growth rates: for sales, expenses, employees, etc.
- financial ratio values: for return on investment, inventory turns
- percentage profit margins: gross profit margin targets for major products.

Industry sources can provide financial ratios typical for firms you are competing against. Two sources that can be helpful in uncovering industry financial ratios are FAME (Financial Analysis Made Easy) and Amadeus (analysis of major databases from European sources). Both are CD-ROMs that are produced by Bureaus Van Dijk (their telephone number in the UK is 0171 839 2266). Most business school libraries would have them.

Cash Flow and Budget Projections

Budget projections are very important to an Angel—these are the hard edge of business. They also provide an easy guide to measure your success a year from the initial investment—did you achieve the budget? In the budget you should include a cash flow budget and a capital expenditures budget; pro forma financial statements should be developed based on these. Pro forma statements are financial statements that are prepared as if the events had taken place—they help an Angel see what the position of the business should be at a point in the future. A cash flow budget is the planning document where you estimate the financial resources (cash and credit) needed to carry out planned operations and remain solvent. They can be long term or short term. Long-term cash planning usually covers from three to five years and the pro forma financial statements are used to develop it; short-term covers one year and these detailed projections are made through a cash budget.

A cash budget is a period-by-period estimate of the amount of timing of the cash inflows (receipts) and outflows (disbursements) associated with your future operations. The budget is usually for one year, divided up into monthly or weekly budget intervals. The estimates of these flows consist of:

- cash receipts from normal operations—this includes receipts from cash sales plus collection of accounts receivable
- the cash receipts from non-operating sources, such as the sale of a fixed asset or a tax refund

- the cash disbursements associated with normal operations, including the payments for purchases (accounts payable) and payments for cash operating expenses such as payroll and taxes
- cash disbursements associated with fixed asset purchases, repayment of debt obligations, and the payment of dividends.

SUMMARY

This chapter is an important one for every entrepreneur because a sound business plan is an important key to bringing funding sources on board and, perhaps even more importantly, the discipline of thoroughly preparing a business plan helps minimise the possibility of failure and substantially increases the likelihood of success of a fledgling venture.

NOTES

1. Some Business Link offices deal only with established firms and for a start-up you may need to turn to an Enterprise Agency.
2. This section draws on Abrams, 1993.
3. This section uses ideas from DeThomas and Fredenberger, 1995.
4. For those in new industries, a good book to help you think about these types of issues is *Competing For the Future* by Gary Hamel and C.K. Prahalad (1996). Gary Hamel teaches at the London Business School and provides some good European examples of emerging and dramatically transforming industries.
5. We have tried to provide the average entrepreneur with sufficient detail in this section to enable them to write their own venture's business plan. If you would like further information on the five forces framework, consult Michael Porter's (1980), *Competitive Strategy*.
6. The term mass customisation was first brought to public attention by Joseph Pine with his book *Mass Customization: The New Frontier in Business Competition*. There is a more recent article by Gilmore and Pine in the January, 1997 *Harvard Business Review*. The decline of the relative importance of economies of scale has proponents on both sides: see an article by Suresh Kotha (1995) in the *Strategic Management Journal*, or for the other side, one by Sharon Oswald and William Boulton (1995) in the *California Management Review*. The conclusion may be similar to the conclusion reached concerning globalisation potential: it is best to think of the idea at the industry level—for this discussion see George Yip's (1995) book, *Total Global Strategy*.
7. The Internet has proven to be an interesting new channel of distribution for some small firms, especially in the software field, where they can offer global distribution of their software via downloading directly to the customer's PC. This is one of the few industries that has really taken off on the Internet, but the potential is there for many industries. New articles on how to compete successfully on the Net come out almost monthly now, and the playing field is moving so rapidly you really do need to keep up to date with the latest tactics. However, a good article to start with is "Who will be the big winners on the Internet?", by Karl Moore and Ben Andradi

(1996), and a good starting book is *Customer Service on the Internet* by Jim Sterne (1996).

8. An excellent book that discusses high-tech product life cycles is, *Inside the Tornado* by Geoffrey Moore (1995).

9. The only good book we are aware of on effectively competing in declining markets is Kathryn Harrigan's (1980) *Strategies for Declining Businesses.* We can also recommend her article with Michael Porter (1983), "End game strategies for declining industries".

10. Here we follow Cooper (1993) and define a new product if it has been on the market by a firm for five years or less.

11. A December 1996 *Business Week* article outlined the continued improvement in the density and price of computer chips, the underlying technology driving the knowledge economy we live in.

12. An excellent book on hypercompetitive markets is *Hypercompetition* by Richard Avendi (1994).

13
The Six Phases
of Company Financing

From the time an entrepreneurial idea is born and takes its first steps in the real world as a business venture, it has many challenges ahead and many obstacles to avoid. With the parental care of an experienced entrepreneur, the venture may initially be guided over the rocky road to prosperity, but all too often the entrepreneur is a first time parent and more help is needed as the venture grows. There are many sources of guidance, such as business introduction services (see Chapter 14), regional business TECs (Training and Enterprise Councils), professional business advisers and numerous books on how to start and run a business. But none of these is fully comprehensive.

In this chapter we present a new model, based on a more established and proven framework, developed by a prominent academic in the field of entrepreneurship, Neil Churchill (Churchill, 1997; Churchill and Lewis, 1983). This describes six key phases of company growth. Here we apply these phases specifically to the problems of procuring company financing (when internally generated funds are not enough) and analyse the financing obstacles at each stage of a venture's development. In our opinion, this is another guide, although more financially based, which can be beneficial to any person pondering or implementing an entrepreneurial idea.

THE MODEL

In his model, Churchill describes the key phases of company growth and the different challenges that each stage presents as a small firm grows. Identifying each phase independently and scrutinising it may yield much insight on the challenges and potential problems a firm might experience as it grows from a one-person firm into, possibly, a large incorporated firm. Although these stage

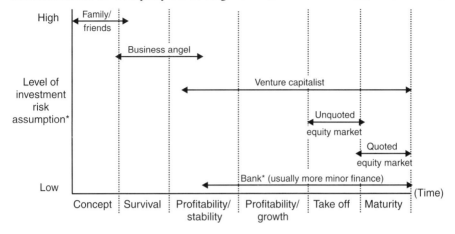

Figure 13.1 sums up the findings that we describe in the rest of the chapter. As you can see, different finance providers can be courted depending on the development stage and risk level of the firm.

Figure 13.1 A typology of different external investor types
Source: Adapted from van Osnabrugge (1998)

transitions will not be alike in every firm, market, industry, or region of the country, the framework is useful and has many potential applications. Churchill found that the model was "deemed by several hundred owner/managers to be useful in helping them assess what skills and resources were needed both for the present and the future. Owners who can assess the stage at which their companies are operating can use the framework to understand better existing problems and anticipate future challenges." In the same manner, we hope that our "financing-specific" addition to his model will be of practical value to those thinking of starting an entrepreneurial venture.

Figure 13.1 sums up the findings that we describe in the rest of the chapter. As you can see, different finance providers can be courted depending on the development stage and risk level of the firm.

We'll now examine each stage in depth to determine why different finance providers are prominent in the different phases of company growth.

STAGE 1: CONCEPTION/EXISTENCE

In this stage the company is still on the drawing-board—it has yet to become a business entity. Churchill states that typically the firm:

- is still somewhat conceptual
- has not solved the problem of obtaining customers, or it cannot deliver the product or service contracted for in the necessary quantity or with the necessary quality
- has a simple organisation structure—the owner does everything and directly supervises subordinates, who in the main are of average competence
- has minimal to non-existent systems and formal planning
- has a simple strategy—to survive.

Financing

The financing options at this stage are the entrepreneur's savings, family and friends. Since the concept or, if it has already been born, the start-up company is in such an early stage of development, it has very high inherent risk. Its products, services, market and customer base have not been proven and it is difficult to gauge the probability of the venture's survival and possible success. With such high risks and no collateral, banks are not in a position to lend money to such projects and Business Angels are often wary of getting involved before any true potential can be seen.

In such cases, when there is no company track record and no collateral, what motivates investors to give financial backing are the market potential of the product, and the track record and personal qualities of the entrepreneur. However, at this stage of development, the product's market potential (assuming the product has already been produced) will not yet have been tested in the market and its potential is speculative at best. Furthermore, few entrepreneurs have the necessary industry track records to encourage a Business Angel or venture capitalist to invest in such a risky venture and such an unproven idea. Some Business Angels may invest, but they usually like to see more proof on the viability of the business and the entrepreneur. The saving grace for such young firms are usually the friends and relatives of the entrepreneur, who know the personal qualities of the firm's founder and give financing based on trust and confidence, or because they feel they have an obligation to do so. With such personal incentives for investment, family and friends might not be the most rational investors and may not conduct much due diligence on the entrepreneurial venture—assuming their personal knowledge and trust might suffice for research.

These family and friends are usually the last resort for the entrepreneur when his or her savings have been depleted. Although many of today's large firms were initially founded with financial support from family and friends, there are many more firms that have gone under and in the process lost the funds that family and friends worked so hard to earn. Thus, if things don't go as planned, there is potential for severe friction between a firm's owner and those close to him or her. Although an entrepreneur must bear this possibility in mind before accepting help from family and friends, many people have little option but to turn to this source of funding.

STAGE 2: SURVIVAL

In this stage the business has proven that the main product is viable and that the firm will survive, but there is some uncertainty as to whether the firm will be able to grow and start generating sizeable returns. These firms are often "life-style businesses", which have limited growth potential but certainly can be sustained at a minimal profit for as long as the entrepreneur is willing to put in the required effort. Churchill states:

> The key problem thus shifts from mere existence to the relationship between revenues and expenses. The main issues are as follows:
>
> (1) In the short run, can we generate enough cash to break even and to cover the repair or replacement of our capital assets as they wear out?
>
> (2) Can we, at a minimum, generate enough cash flow to stay in business and to finance growth to a size that is sufficiently large, given our industry and market niche, to earn an economic return on our assets and labour?

Some firms manage to grow past this stage into profitability, but many remain as "ma and pa stores" and just survive without further growth.

Financing

In this stage the business has proven that it can survive and may have the potential to grow further. The initial risks and doubts about the viability of the entrepreneurial idea have lessened and this might well attract others to invest. The entrepreneur will usually have exhausted his or her personal savings and also the financial generosity of family and friends, while banks may still be reluctant to take on such high-risk investment proposals without the necessary assets as collateral. Generally, it is not until the firm has a more solid track record and greater stability that banks will be willing to extend a helping hand.

With still little solidity and no profit, the business is of little attraction to venture capitalists, who usually prefer something at a later stage, when it is more secure and with higher growth prospects and larger financial requirements. Furthermore, such small firm investments are not economical for the venture capitalist; just the due diligence and transaction costs may well amount to a large percentage of the investment sought. Often such small investments are not cost-effective and are too burdensome for the large venture capital investor.

One type of investor who does not shy away from filling this "equity gap"—where firms are too small to attract venture capital finance and too risky to attract bank finance—are wealthy private individuals who often invest in these ventures for fun, or to lend their managerial expertise to a growing venture. Business Angels are the perfect addition to these struggling small firms. With their managerial experience, they can render valuable assistance and guide the growth of the firm, and their managerial input is often as valuable as their financial one.

But if these firms are still high risk, why should Business Angels invest? One answer might be that the money these Angels put into the firm is often "casino money" to them—if they lose it, it will probably not affect their standard of living. So why not invest it in a business venture that will possibly give them a great deal of satisfaction and high returns? Another reason might be that in growing entrepreneurial firms, the early stages of development (when the equity is still not valued too highly) might be the only time when Business Angels can afford to invest. As the company grows, the equity gains in value and the ability to buy a sizeable equity percentage (with which an investor has some say in the running of the firm) may be more limited.

STAGE 3: PROFITABILITY/STABILISATION

In this stage, Churchill states:

> The company has attained true economic health, has sufficient size and product-market penetration to ensure economic success and earns average or above average profits. The company can stay at this stage indefinitely provided environmental change does not destroy its market niche or ineffective management reduces its competitive abilities.

The company is now in a position to recruit more management and the cash income stream is plentiful. But the main concern is that these cash flows are substantial enough to be retained for possible uncertain periods ahead. With a more profitable income statement, more formal procedures (i.e. accounting, marketing, etc.) are being adopted to ease the firm's transition to higher sales and greater commitments. To ensure continued success, the firm will have to continue to adapt to environment changes, its failure to do so could see a return of the firm to the survival stage.

Financing

Although the firm has finally started to earn a positive cash flow and is profitable at this stage, there is probably not enough financial capital to finance growth. Although further growth is still not such a concern at this stage and the financial demands from outside investors not too great, the entrepreneur may wish to start securing some financial backing to enable future growth in later stages. Since profitability and stability may be the two most important criteria at this stage, securing capital for potential expansion may thus strategically be wise if an avenue of growth is chosen for the firm. Many firms in this stage may elect to remain here or may falter and return to the survival stage. But those firms who wish, and are able, to continue their expansion will most likely be interested in acquiring support for such future growth.

Financing at this stage is on the upper financial edge of the classical "equity gap". At this stage Business Angels are no longer the principal source of financial capital. Many might still be interested in investing, but the firm may now be too large (and its equity too expensive) for the average wealthy private individual to acquire an influential stake. However, some more risk-averse and more passive investors may wish to enter such a financing deal for a small percentage of equity.

As in the last stage, banks may be interested in lending small, collateral-secured, loans, but these would probably not be in the region of funding levels the company is seeking for its possible expansion plans. The more the company grows and decreases its inherent entrepreneurial risks, the more comfortable the banks may be in lending larger sums of secured loans.

In stage three, formal venture capital becomes the main form of new financing sought. The majority of venture capital firms wish to invest only in firms with almost unlimited growth potential, and firms in this stage can offer exactly that. These firms have proven their marketability and their product demand, they are starting to turn a profit, and with the right amount of guidance and financial backing some of them have the potential to experience sizeable growth. With high financial returns as the principal investment motive, venture capitalists have a greater chance of attaining their investment goals through investment in a firm at this stage of development than in a firm at a less developed and less proven stage. Thus, although firms in this phase might be on the higher end of the scale of risk that venture capitalists are willing to assume, the sizeable potential that many of these firms can offer may warrant the investment risk.

STAGE 4: PROFITABILITY/GROWTH

In this stage, Churchill says,

> The owner-manager consolidates the company and marshals resources for growth. He takes the cash and the established borrowing power of the company and puts it to risk to finance growth. The important tasks include making sure

the business stays profitable . . . and to hire and develop managers of a higher quality than those needed to run a stable company.

With continued growth, the company must start to plan more strategically and assume better systems for production and control. If the firm handles these pressures well, then it has the potential to grow into the next stage, the take-off stage. If the firm is not fully committed to growth, then it may return to the previous stage with potentially a less prosperous future.

Financing

As in the last stage, outside financial capital is still not too critical, although it must be secured if the company wishes to progress to the next stage of evolution. The size of the financing needs in this stage will continue to exceed what the average Business Angel is willing to invest. The Corporate Business Angels may be interested in buying share equity, but as the firm becomes more valuable, this becomes less likely. More passive Business Angels might be interested in investing, but this is less common than in previous stages of company development.

Bank finance is still an option (especially now that the firm is stronger financially and has a larger asset base upon which to borrow), but it still presents limitations. The financial amounts that a company would be able to borrow from a bank on its asset base may not be enough to finance its intended growth, although it may be sufficient to finance temporary cash flow concerns and asset purchases.

In this stage, as in the last, formal venture capital is the main source of outside funding. More so than in the last stage, firms now need to secure more substantial sums of financial backing to support the expansion and growth that the next phase of firm evolution can bring. Without this backing, the firm will most likely have to remain in this stage, for its own profits will not be sufficient to finance its expansion plans. With the firm on the verge of a growth phase, assuming it has the potential to do so, venture capital firms will be very interested in getting involved. With expertise in the industrial sector and experience in guiding the expansion of entrepreneurial firms, venture capitalists can render non-financial assistance as well as financial. But certain considerations are also present for the entrepreneur when seeking such out-side financial assistance.

The entrepreneur should assess the amount of equity and control he or she is willing to surrender to the venture capitalists to finance growth. If too much equity is diluted from the entrepreneur's share, the incentive and motivational effects for the entrepreneur may also be diluted and this could cause problems for the investors, the firm and the management. However, most venture cap-italists are experienced in such investment situations and will often allow the entrepreneur to retain control, acting as more of a passive adviser on the board of the company, and electing only to get actively involved if it is really needed by the venture. Thus, at this phase of company development venture capital is the most likely option of financing.

STAGE 5: TAKE OFF

In this stage, Churchill says, "the key problem is determining how to achieve rapid growth and how to finance it. The most important problems that then follow are delegation, cash management, and cost control." The firm now has many growth pressures and the over-worked management may be concentrating on more micro areas of firm management (e.g. hiring, sales), rather than on the bigger picture, maybe to the extent that the overall macro variables may not be scrutinised as closely as they should.

Churchill says:

> This is a pivotal period in a company's life. If the owner rises to the challenge of a growing company, both financially and managerially, it can become a big business. If not, it can usually be sold—at a profit—provided the owner recognises his or her limitations soon enough. Too often, those who bring the business through the previous stages are unsuccessful in stage 5, either because they try to grow too fast and run out of cash (the owner falls victim to the omnipotence syndrome) or are unable to delegate (the omniscience syndrome).

By this stage, the role of the original entrepreneur may still have great influence in the running of the firm, but in some situations, the entrepreneur might have been replaced by the shareholders of the company, with a new management team installed to handle the pressures of expansion and growth. There is some debate as to whether entrepreneurs that start small firms are also able managers (and make sound decisions) when the firm has reached a large size. Examples of both can be found in abundance.

Financing

In this stage outside finance becomes critical as the firm plans to expand and grow. As in the previous two stages, formal venture capital is the most prominent form of financial support, although unlike in the previous two stages, the financing is now of much greater concern and must be secured if the firm is to grow further. At this phase of development, the risks are still quite high and there is great need for outside management expertise. Banks remain a doubtful option due to their constraining lending rules, which cannot permit the lending of the sizeable amount needed for the company's growth in this stage. Luckily, venture capitalists excel in this area of finance. They have experience in such industry-specific growth opportunities and often recruit a more balanced management team for the venture.

An additional funding option arises at this stage of a firm's growth: the Alternative Investment Market (AIM) or the OFEX market. Both markets deal in the shares on unquoted ventures (with the latter handling stocks that are generally smaller than those of the former) and may present an alternative mode of finance for those firms that cannot secure venture capital, but still desire financial backing for expansion. In this phase of development, these firms are more stable and less risky than start-up ventures, but still much less so than those on the large, quoted markets. The risks on these unquoted markets are higher, but the expected returns are higher as well. Although these markets are not as "efficient" as the larger, quoted equity markets, they certainly offer more efficiency to those developing firms seeking financial capital to foster further growth.

STAGE 6: MATURITY

For firms in the mature stage, according to Churchill, "the greatest concerns of a company are, first, to consolidate and control the financial gains brought on by rapid growth and, second, to retain the advantages of small size, including flexibility of response and the entrepreneurial spirit." To contain the growth experienced, the firm must adopt professional tools such as budgets and strategies to enable the growing workforce to effectively run the sizeable firm. The systems are well developed and the staff professional. But unlike in past phases, "the owner and the business are quite separate, both financially and operationally. The company has now arrived." The most substantial problem now becomes the challenge of preserving the entrepreneurial qualities that built the firm and may enable it to remain competitive in a dynamic market.

Financing

Financing is still of great concern at this stage, although certainly not as crucial as in the previous growth stage. Now that the company has matured and stabilised, bank financing may be sufficient to finance its cash and acquisition needs, but at such a developed stage many firms elect to go public. Through flotation the firm can attain substantial trading value, generating the long-awaited financial profits for the entrepreneur and the exit routes that many of the investors (Business Angels and venture capitalists alike) have been waiting for. Going public is often the last major financing option an entrepreneurial firm undertakes as it grows into a large and mature business concern.

SUMMARY

As the entrepreneurial venture evolves from one growth stage to the next, its requirements for external financing change (if the firm cannot supply enough funds internally) and so do the investors who are willing to fill those financing needs. According to Churchill's model, the company evolves through six stages. In this chapter we have applied these stages specifically to the financing needs and options of the developing firm. In the *conception stage (stage 1)* the cash needs are great, as are the risks, and we find that the entrepreneur's own financial wealth, as well as the financial contributions from family and friends, primarily supports the venture.

Then, as the firm enters the *survival stage (stage 2)* it has demonstrated its viability, but the risks and financing requirements are still high. In this stage, Business Angels fill the classical "equity gap", where the firm is too risky and asset-free to warrant bank lending, and the size of the funds demanded are too small for the traditional formal venture capitalist.

In the next stage, the *profitability/stabilisation stage (stage 3)*, the company is stabilised and is, for the first time, generating a profit. At this stage the financing needs have dropped dramatically and the firm is just trying to "find its feet" as it adjusts to profitability and builds a stronger foundation for possible future growth. In this stage, the entrepreneur may wish to start securing financial backing for possible future expansion. Although Business Angel capital may still be an option, venture capital is becoming the more viable and frequent option as the size of the investment amounts sought increases.

The *profitability/growth stage (stage 4)* marshals in a renewed concentration on possible company growth. The firm is still profitable, but there may be concern for laying a foundation for future expansion and thus a need to secure financial backing. At this stage, venture capital becomes even more fundamental and its presence can render a strong platform from which to make the next move: rapid growth.

Deciding how rapidly the firm should grow becomes the chief concern in the *take off stage (stage 5)* and financing requirements are crucial. For the firm to enter this stage, it must have had secured venture capital finance in stage 4. Clearly, formal venture capital finance remains prominent in this stage. But financial backing is not the only advantage a venture capitalist's presence can render. Like Business Angels, venture capitalists can lend the managerial expertise and knowledge of the market to assist the rapid growth of the firm. At this stage there is also one other financing option that might offer benefits: the unquoted stock market. This market is intended for those firms that have growth potential but whose risks are still too great (and whose future too uncertain) to warrant a listing on the quoted exchange.

In the last stage, the *maturity stage (stage 6)*, the level of financing sought is less than that in the previous stage, but can still be quite sizeable as the firm attempts to stabilise and adopt more formal rules to ensure smooth daily operation. With such changes, care should be taken that the firm retains some of its entrepreneurial spirit so that it may be more adaptive to the competitive and dynamic marketplace. When a firm has reached this stage, it is usually quite large and its best option may be to get quoted on a formal stock exchange. Going public would provide the exit routes that many of the investors have been seeking. Such a transaction is often the best, if not the only, way for Business Angel and venture capitalist investors to realise the capital gains they have accumulated on their entrepreneurial investments.

NOTE

1. This chapter is by Mark van Osnabrugge and Karl Moore. This overview of types of external financiers is adapted from van Osnabrugge (1998).

PART IV
Where Angels Tread

14
Business Introduction Services

One of the biggest problems facing entrepreneurs is finding an appropriate Business Angel. We hope this book has helped you understand the various types of Angels and to find one which matches your venture's needs the best. For Angels a key issue that our research uncovered was finding the "right" opportunities. In this chapter we explain the different types of resources that are available to entrepreneurs (as a means of finding potential investors) and to Business Angels (as a means of finding a suitable investment opportunity that matches their investment criteria).[1]

In the final section of the chapter we also provide a listing of venture capital firms that will consider investing less than £100 000. Venture capital firms act as principals, and manage institutional or in-house money they invest in un-quoted companies. The investment criteria and the process of raising finance may be more rigorous than for a Business Angel.

THE INFORMAL VENTURE CAPITAL MARKET

Unlike the market for formal venture capital, the market for Business Angel financing has often been called a hidden or invisible market (see Wetzel, 1987) where the best channels for communication between entrepreneurs and potential investors are often lacking. Because most Business Angels prefer anonymity, they are difficult to identify and this restricts the ability of entrepreneurs to identify them. Likewise, Business Angels say that they have problems finding sufficient investment opportunities that match their invest-ment criteria. This might be due to the fact for most investors these types of investments are just a spare-time activity and considerable time is required to search for and appraise investment opportunities (Harrison and Mason, 1995). Thus, most Business Angels tend to rely on their friends, accountants,

legal advisers and business associates for referrals on investment opportunities that might match their interests.

In our experience, there is a considerable need for more formal channels of
communication between Business Angels and entrepreneurs. This void is
partially filled by business introduction services (BISs), also known as business angel networks (BANs).

THE ROLE OF BUSINESS INTRODUCTION SERVICES

Business introduction services attempt to increase the efficiency of communication between entrepreneurs and Business Angels. They do this by
making the Business Angels more visible and accessible for entrepreneurs,
and by minimising the search costs of finding an attractive investment opportunity for Business Angels. They usually function only as a means of
introduction and not as dealers or investment advisers. They also tend to
avoid participating in the negotiations between entrepreneurs and Business
Angels.[2]

The most conventional method for introduction these services offer is the
publication of a monthly magazine of investment opportunities in which
entrepreneurs (for a small fee) can feature their businesses. This magazine
is then distributed by the BIS to a large number of Business Angels on
subscription.

There are many benefits to this approach:

- an entrepreneur may advertise a business to a wide audience of potential
  investors simultaneously
- the benefit for Business Angels is that they can retain their anonymity while
  they scrutinise various investment opportunities, without the obligation to
  divulge their identity until negotiations become imminent
- the subscribers (i.e. Business Angels) and the entrepreneurs have to pay a
  fee to, respectively, receive and be featured in the magazine, which helps to
  filter out those who are not serious about investing or building up a firm
- the search costs of all parties involved are considerably less than they would
  otherwise be without these channels of communication.

DIFFERENT TYPES OF BUSINESS INTRODUCTION SERVICES

There are many different types of BISs. Richard Harrison and Colin Mason,
prominent UK researchers into the informal venture capital market, have

identified three distinctions of BIS.[3] We will look at these here, and add a fourth type to make the list more complete.

Which is best for you? Well, it depends on your needs. Why there are four types of BISs is because there can be considerable differences in needs between various types of entrepreneurs and Angels. A careful analysis to understand your needs, whether as an entrepreneur or an Angel, is an important first step to choosing the best business introduction service for you. We suggest you read through the following descriptions to determine which type of BIS is appropriate for you, and then contact several of the BISs that seem to fit your needs to help you decide which of those seems to have the best approach in your circumstances. Brief descriptions of BISs operating in the UK are given after the following explanations of the different types.

Local vs. National Services

Most BISs operate on a regional/local scale, providing services to a population of typically 1–2 million. These tend to be government sponsored initiatives. As you can see from Table 14.1, there are many regional services around the UK. In addition to these business introduction services, there are also two other government-sponsored services available to entrepreneurs and Business Angels. The first are local enterprise agencies, which primarily provide start-up business counselling. The second, and the more prominent, are TECs or Business Links, which provide a much broader range of services for entrepreneurial firms. If you wish to find out more about a TEC or Business Link service in your area (there are 81 TECs and 89 Links nationwide), you can call the National Business Link Signpost Line on tel. 0345 567765. We provide further information on TECs later in this chapter under the Business Link Network entry.

All other BISs in the market provide services nationwide. Two of the more established in this area are Venture Capital Report (VCR) and Local Investment Networking Company (LINC). VCR is the oldest business introduction service in the UK and matches entrepreneurs and Business Angels through their monthly investors' magazine and investment presentations. They also provide a workshop to help both entrepreneurs and investors. VCR is a private, for-profit business which has successfully raised more than £16 million nationally for about 190 companies over the last 19 years. LINC is a government-sponsored service which also uses magazine matching and investment presentation approaches for its clients and it claims to have raised £10 million nationally since its inception. However, LINC is actually a federation of 12 smaller local business introduction services, so it might also be considered as a local service provider.

Public Sector Agencies vs. Private Agencies

Most local services receive financial support from public sector agencies and usually only offer the conventional matchmaking service through an investment opportunity magazine, and in some cases investment clubs. Harrison and Mason (1995) point out that "these networks are prevented by securities legislation from having an involvement in the post-introduction deal-making process".

In the arena of private business introduction services, there are two main types. The first group are "conventional" matching services, which use investor opportunities magazines (e.g. Venture Capital Report) and computer matching (e.g. Venture Net) to locate suitable investors for the entrepreneurial investment opportunities they feature. The second group of private business introduction services tend to be "offshoots" from large financial service companies. These offshoots usually have larger minimum investment requirement levels and tend also to charge a success fee.

Types of Matching Mechanisms Used

Conventional or Classic Approach

This approach dominates over all others. It utilises the conventional techniques (such as distributing an investors' magazine with investment opportunities) to introduce entrepreneurial ventures to potential investors.

Ancillary Service Approach

This approach specialises in matching experienced business people with companies that have strategic gaps in their management teams. They may also lend their own management expertise to assist the running of entrepreneurial ventures. This service may appeal to experienced professionals who wish to invest in an unquoted firm and also wish to be very actively involved in its day-to-day running.

Institutional Arch Angels Approach

Institutional arch angels are companies that identify, screen and structure investment opportunities on behalf of their syndicate of Business Angel investors. The Business Angels will usually be expected to take a passive role in the investment, although some firms may be able to match a Business Angel's

Table 14.1 Composition of Business Introduction Services in the UK (1997)

Public, not for profit, conventional matching	Private, for profit, conventional matching	Private, for profit, institutional arch angel (lead investors)	Private for profit, ancillary services (Interim management)	Invention services
Local/regional				
Business Link Gloucestershire	A14 Angels (Midlands)		Solutions for Scotland	
Business Link Hereford & Worcester	The Business Angels Bureau (Midlands)		Talisman Ventures*	
Business Link Investors Network (East Anglia)	The Enterprise Forum (Norfolk & Suffolk)			
Business Link Network (central link to 160+ regional business support services around UK)	Greater Eastern Investment Forum (East Anglia) Halo (South) Mercantile 100 (mostly Scotland) WINSEC Corporate			
Capital Access (Manchester)	Exchange (E. Anglia)*			
Capital Connections (East Lancashire)	Yorkshire Association of Business Angels			
The Capital Market (Milton Keynes & N. Bucks)				
Capital Match (W. Sussex)				
Cheshire Contacts*				
Entrust (North-East)				
EquityLink (Hertford)				
EquityLink (Kent)				
Informal Register of Investment Services (West Yorkshire)				
LentA Ventures (London)				
LINC Scotland				
Oxfordshire Investment Opportunity Network				
South West Investment Group (Devon & Cornwall)				
TECHINVEST (Cheshire)				
National				
LINC (Local Investment Networking Company)	Beer & Partners* Blackstone Franks & Co* Daily Telegraph Business Network* Hilling Wall Corporate Finance* IDJ Ltd* Independent Private Equity Company NatWest Angels Service Principality Financial Management* Venture Capital Report VentureNet	Corbett Keeling*	Cambridge Venture Management Cavendish Management Resources Dunstable Management Group	Inventions Isis Innovation

Source: Adapted by M. van Osnabrugge from: BVCA (1993, 1994), Harrison and Mason (1995).
Note: *Not exclusively involved in Business Angel finance.

experience and preferences with an unquoted firm. Venture capital firms have also started to enter this area of informal venture capital investment and have created funds in which Business Angels can invest.

Invention Introduction Services

To the types of business introduction services mentioned above, we will add a fourth type: those services that advise entrepreneurs/investors on how best to exploit the full potential of their product inventions. They counsel and advise on patent protection, licensing and on how to commercialise an invention. These firms usually take a percentage of the royalties as their fee.

The next section contains a comprehensive listing of the business introduction services available in the UK at the time of writing. Table 14.1 places each service in its relevant category: locally or nationally concentrated, publicly or privately funded, matching approach used, and whether it specialises in exploitation of product inventions.

LISTING OF UK BUSINESS INTRODUCTION SERVICES

In the rest of this chapter, we list and give a brief description of the business introduction services operating in the UK.

Most of the data given here has been provided to us by the individual business introduction services and they are responsible for the accuracy of their statements. In addition, we referred to the British Venture Capital Association's *Sources of Business Angel Capital 1996/97* for some of the information for "Investment £ sought", "No. of investors" and "Successful matches". The authors' summary was added by us. If you would like to obtain more detailed information on these business introduction services, please contact them directly or see one of the other Business Angel service guides available: The *BVCA Guide*, or *The Venture Capital Report Guide to Venture Capital in the UK and Europe*.[4]

No responsibility can be accepted by the authors for the accuracy or any action taken or not taken as a result of information contained in this chapter. Specific advice should always be taken in each situation from your financial or legal adviser.

A14 Angels

Bill Smart/Richard Joyce
Capital & Commercial Finance Ltd
Whitecroft House
8 Cloister Crofts
Royal Leamington Spa
Warwickshire CV32 6QQ

Tel.: 01926 330196
Fax: 01926 339800

Date of formation: 1995
Organisation type: Private—investment
*   opportunities*
Geographical area: Midlands/East Anglia
Matching methods: One-on-one meetings
Investment £ sought: £10 000–£250 000
No. of investors: 46
Successful matches (July 1995–June 1996): 4
Industry preferences: All
Stage of investment: All
Additional services: Full corporate finance
*   services*

Authors' Summary

A14 Angels is a business introduction service which uses personal introductions and investor meetings to match entrepreneurial companies seeking finance with potential investors in the Midlands and East Anglia area. They also offer a full range of corporate finance services to local businesses.

Company Literature

Covering the Midlands and East Anglia areas (the A14 corridor), A14 Angels uses personal introductions, one-to-one meetings and investor meetings to match small firms seeking finance with investors.

To be included in the service, companies must have a good quality business plan and a proposal supported by management or audited accounts where applicable. Investors registered with the service should show evidence that they have the ability to invest.

The typical company using A14 Angels to find Business Angel financing is seeking £10 000–£250 000 in funding and is usually in the early stages of development. However, firms in all stages, and in all industry sectors are welcome to utilise the service, as long as they have a viable and realistic business plan and a willingness to give up part of their equity base to fund growth.

In addition to providing informal equity services, this introduction service also offers full corporate finance assistance to local businesses.

The following is a more detailed list of their non-Angel services:

- non-executive database
- interim management service
- full corporate finance facilities
- executive search and selection

The cost for companies seeking finance is £150–£250 per annum, and £50 for registered investors seeking investment opportunities.

Beer & Partners

David Beer
Beer & Partners
The Bell House
West Street
Dorking
Surrey RH4 1BS

Tel.: 01306 742104
Fax: 01306 742101

Date of formation: 1995
Organisation type: Private equity advisers
Geographical area: UK, mostly London,
   South-East and South
Matching methods: Personal introductions
Investment £ sought: £50 000+
No. of investors: 150
Successful matches (July 1995–June 1996): 9
Industry preferences: All
Stage of investment: All
Additional services: Full range of business
   services

Authors' Summary

Beer & Partners offers a personal business introduction service based on close knowledge of the investors. In addition to business introductions, they offer a full range of services crucial to small firms. They operate throughout the UK, but primarily in the South-East.

Company Literature

Beer & Partners is an active private equity adviser, which accesses a wide range of investors—institutional and private—for clients seeking venture capital. Our particular strength is our close contacts among Business Angels, who look to us to identify investment opportunities with an outlet for their skills and experience.

Our Successes

We completed 22 equity transactions in the year to 30 June 1996, typically between £50 000 and £500 000 capital, for a wide range of clients. This represented a success rate of about two-thirds. Recent examples include:

- £150 000 Carriage Museum, Berkshire
- £900 000 Perimeter Security, Surrey
- £80 000 Engineering, Kent

These figures do not include any secured lending through our extensive banking contacts.

Our People

David Beer CA, ACID is the Principal—former Director of BZW and Westpac, with 30 years' corporate finance experience. He is supported by professional staff with industry and investment experience.

Service for Companies

We will provide an initial review of the business with an assessment of viability, to determine whether we believe we can help. Then follows an examination of the business plan, funding structure and management so that we are able to select the most appropriate investor. The process is geared towards introducing investors to clients as quickly as possible. We then support our client in negotiations with investors and lenders, until conclusion.

Services for Investors

So much time can be wasted in searching for the right business, and our detailed review process is geared to the needs of investors; all of us have, after all, invested in the past. We do not give investment advice.

Our Fees

These are borne by our investee client, and are success related. Any additional work is charged on a time basis and is estimated in advance.

Blackstone Franks & Co.

David Tate/R. Young
Attn: Business Angels
Blackstone Franks & Co.
Barbican House
26–34 Old Street
London EC1V 9HL

Date of formation: 1990
Organisation type: Private—accounting
Geographical area: UK
Matching methods: Investor newsletter and
  computer matching
Investment £ sought: £150 000+
No. of investors: 750
Successful matches (July 1995–June 1996):
  10
Industry preferences: None
Stage of investment: All

Tel.: 0171 250 3300
Fax: 0171 250 1402

Additional services: Advice and business
  plan formulation

Authors' Summary

Blackstone Franks & Co. is a chartered accounting firm established in 1976. It started its Business Angels service in 1990 and is able to render assistance from the first instance of seeking finance to the formulation of an investment agreement.

Company Literature

Blackstone Franks maintains a free database of wealthy private individuals who have expressed a desire to make a Business Angel investment. On a regular basis, Blackstone Franks will compile a list of investment opportunities and acquisitions and distributes it to everyone on the database. This is augmented by a computer matching service, which strives to match firms with the preferences and managerial skills of the investors.

Before a company can be featured on the distribution list, Blackstone Franks must be pleased with the content and the management of the venture.

The cost of this service is completely free to investors. The charge to firms seeking to raise finance is often negotiable, depending on time and success. A success fee is levied on a decreasing basis should the firm raise funding from an investor on the Blackstone Franks database.

The management team at Blackstone Franks consists of professionals with many years of industry expertise and specialist expertise in an array of areas, such as MBOs of businesses from local authorities and search assignments for acquisition and buy-in.

The Business Angels Bureau Ltd

Bob Barnsley
The Business Angels Bureau Ltd
60 Worcester Street
Stourbridge
West Midlands DY8 1AS

Tel.: 01384 443535
Fax: 01384 440984

Date of formation: 1994
Organisation type: Private—publisher of
investment opportunities
Geographical area: UK (primarily
Midlands)
Matching methods: Publish bulletins
Investment £ sought: £10 000–£1 million
No. of investors: 52
Successful matches (July 1995–June 1996):
3
Industry preferences: All
Stage of investment: All
Additional services: Companies for sale

Authors' Summary

The Business Angels Bureau is a business introduction service which publishes a bi-monthly bulletin of entrepreneurial investment opportunities that gets distributed to a subscriber list of Business Angels. Although it operates primarily in the Midlands, it is starting to spread nationally.

Company Literature

The Business Angels Bureau was established by its members to act as an introduction agency. It successfully matches businesses requiring relatively small amounts of equity capital with private funding from Business Angels. Amounts invested can be as little as £10 000 or as much as £500 000. In fact there is no limit, particularly where the investment can be syndicated.

The directors and advisers at the Business Angels Bureau have a wealth of management and business expertise across a diverse range of industries. The Business Angels Bureau does not just provide another database of business opportunities, but a range of services:

The *Bulletin* is circulated on a subscription basis to an extensive network of investors. It provides a detailed register of companies seeking investment. The information is packaged in such a way as to provide prospective investors with a comprehensive profile of each business in a standard, readable format.

The *Newsletter* is a summary of the *bulletin*. It is circulated to other Angels groups, venture capital funds, banks, accountants, other intermediaries and a variety of people who might have an interest in such investments.

The Network

The investment opportunities contained in the *Bulletin* are also advertised in various appropriate newspapers and periodicals.

Additional Services

The Business Angels Bureau also provides a number of other cost-effective support services on a fixed price "menu" basis. All of these services are provided by qualified people and should considerably improve the chances of raising funding. They can also offer a level of comfort to potential investors.

The objective of the Business Angels Bureau is to provide the framework for dialogue that leads to successful funding. The Bureau enables companies to access potential investors through an extensive, but confidential, database. It offers companies a "menu" of additional cost-effective and complementary services, including due diligence.

Business Link Gloucestershire

Steve Gallagher
Business Link Gloucestershire
Chargrove House Business Centre
Main Road
Shurdington
Cheltenham
Glos GL51 GA

Tel.: 01452 509509/0800 135235
Fax: 01452 509500

Date of formation: 1992
Organisation type: Business Link
Geographical area: Gloucestershire
Matching methods: Investment bulletin
Investment £ sought: £5000–£250 000
No. of investors: 58
Successful matches (July 1995–June 1996):
*   9*
Industry preferences: Manufacturing and
*   engineering*
Stage of investment: Early and expansion
Additional services: Financial advice

Authors' Summary

Supported by the Gloucestershire Enterprise Agency, this business introduction service distributes a bulletin of entrepreneurial investment opportunities to a list of
potential investors. Furthermore, the service also offers a "one stop shop" for business
information and assists firms at every stage of development.

Company Literature

Business Link Gloucestershire is the "one stop shop" for business information, advice
and support for small and medium-sized companies. It is built on a partnership between the Gloucestershire Training and Enterprise Council, the Gloucestershire
Chamber of Commerce and Industry and the County Council.

Business Link provides a range of services and access to information through a team
of highly skilled and experienced business advisers. These are designed to assist local
companies at every stage of their development, and in every area of their business.

Some of the areas where specialist help and/or funding is available include:

- Business counselling service—to provide quality impartial advice to any small or
  medium-sized business to assist with growth.
- Business networking—to encourage small or medium-sized enterprises to collabor-
  ate formally, solve common problems and pursue new business opportunities.
- Business Angels scheme—to provide an introductory service, matching potential
  investors of venture capital with companies seeking private investment.
- Grantfinder service—to facilitate the take up of central government and European
  Community grants and assistance.
- Rescue counselling service—to provide quality advice and guidance to any business
  within the small or medium sized enterprise sector experiencing severe financial
  problems.
- Small firms training loans—to assist firms to borrow the funds needed to pay for a
  training programme.
- Innovation service—provides guidance and support to companies or individuals
  seeking to bring new innovations to the marketplace.
- Step scheme—encourages businesses to provide work experience to second year
  undergraduates.

- Business skills seminars—to provide specific and relevant business skills training for owners and managers of new and established businesses.
- Business start-up scheme—to enable those wishing to start their own business to take advantage of counselling, training and Business Link services.
- Business advisers—to offer independent and impartial advice and support while developing and maintaining a long-term relationship.
- Diagnostic and consultancy service—to help local business to improve their efficiency and competitiveness through external consultancy service.
- Information service—to provide information to support local business including company information checks, product information, financial data, market research and guidance on UK, European Community, exports and overseas legislation.

Business Link Hereford & Worcester

Nick Dobson
Financial Projects Manager
Business Link Hereford & Worcester
Corn Square
Leominster HR6 8LR

Tel.: 01568 616344
Fax: 01568 616355

VC800: 01568 610021
E-mail: Nick.Dobson.@blink.blink-
hereford.btx400.co.uk

Date of formation: 1995
Organisation type: Business Link
Geographical area: Hereford & Worcester
Matching methods: Newsletter and
*   personal introductions*
Investment £ sought: £5000–£100 000
No. of investors: 28
Successful matches (July 1995–June 1996):
*   2*
Industry preferences: Manufacturing,
*   engineering, hi-tech and tourism*
Stage of investment: Established, start-up,
*   rescue and turnaround*
Additional services: Financial advice,
*   training and systems advice*

Authors' Summary

Operating as a business introduction services in Hereford and Worcester, this Business Angels scheme circulates anonymous prospectuses on investment opportunities (usually under £100 000) to a list of registered Angels.

Company Literature

Operating throughout parts of Hereford and Worcester covered by the Hereford and Worcester Chamber of Commerce, Training and Enterprise, the Business Link Hereford & Worcester Business Angels scheme is an informal programme marrying up Hereford and Worcester based companies with private investors who are largely, but by no means exclusively, based locally.

Typical project sizes are between £5 000 and £250 000, with the majority falling below £100 000.

Charges (at the time of writing) are £75 for annual registration for both companies and investors and £150 commission on a successful "marriage".

Companies are matched to potential investors by circulation of an anonymous prospectus on the company to either the whole, or selected parts of, the panel of "Angels". Angels, if interested in a prospectus, respond to the scheme administration, which then arranges meetings and acts as an intermediary if required. Prospectuses are circulated either by newsletter (approximately three-monthly) or individually.

In approximately 18 months of operation, the scheme has made some 30 introductions with a success rate of about 17 per cent.

Business Link Investors Network (BLIN)

John Wright	*Date of formation: 1996*
Business Link Investors Network	*Organisation type: Business Link*
Business Link Norfolk and Waveney	*Geographical area: East Anglia*
112 Barrack Street	*Matching methods: Confidential personal*
Norwich	*introductions*
Norfolk NR3 1TX	*Investment £ sought: £20 000–£1 million*
	No. of investors: 18
	Successful matches (July 1995–June 1996):
	2
	Industry preferences: All
	Stage of investment: All
Tel.: 01603 218218	*Additional services: Advice/counselling*
Fax: 01603 218219	*services*

Authors' Summary

The Business Link Investors Network (BLIN) is a business introduction service that uses a very personalised approach to matching investors and entrepreneurs in the strictest confidence. This personal approach is the only process used—investment presentations and bulletins are not utilised. BLIN operates as a local service in the East Anglia area.

Company Literature

BLIN was established by a Business Angel with 25 years' experience in running his own business. Although its main motive is to promote flow of capital to small manufacturing enterprises in the local East Anglia area, it also operates on the assumption that the provision of private finance is a very personal and confidential matter. The BLIN does not like the breakfast seminar type of function since it may involve a company spending a great deal of time and effort making a presentation to a group which may or may not include genuine investors.

The twin objectives of the Network are to bring investment opportunities to the attention of investors and to provide investors with a convenient and confidential means of examining a range of these investment opportunities. The BLIN gets to know both the investee company and the investors on a personal basis. Investment preferences of investors are identified in some detail. This enables the attention of investors to be brought to opportunities which fall within their interests or which have a particular need for the hands-on skills that the investor can provide. This personalised approach to informal investment is very effective. A newsletter has been circulated but BLIN feels that this is not as effective a medium and does not compare with the response achieved by the personal contact, which reaches almost 100 per cent of referrals progressing on to the next stage, which takes the form of an informal meeting between the two parties.

The majority of the BLIN investors are people who have sold their business and conform with the standard description of "Business Angels". There are a number of investors, most of whom have suffered redundancy, who are prepared to make investments that to all intents and purposes enables them to buy into employment. There is very little reported about this source of investment potential.

Although the BLIN was initially aimed at the local business community, it has and is developing links with other networks and venture capital providers. The Network offers access to a range of investment opportunities available in Norfolk and Waveney, an area that has a proven record of producing innovative companies with high-growth potential. It provides information about businesses which seek investment for expansion and links them to investors to form a mutually rewarding relationship.

The Business Link Investors Network links private investors, entrepreneurs and business support organisations to improve the flow of investment capital and management expertise into start-up and growing companies in the region. The network is based on a partnership between Business Link Norfolk and Waveney and organisations that hold key positions in the economic development of the region and is supported by the Department of Trade and Industry (DTI).

Business Link Network

Organisation type: Government funded referral service for the 89 Business Links and the 81 business TECs in the UK
Geographical area: Referrals to local area business support services in the UK
Service: Support service for entrepreneurs and businesses
Industry preferences: All
Stage of investment: All

Business Link Signpost Line:
Tel.: 0345 567765
(charged as a local call)

Authors' Summary

As the central referral line for all the Business Links and Training and Enterprise Councils (TECs) around the UK, the Business Link Network is a valuable resource for entrepreneurs who want local assistance in starting a company, growing a small firm, or running an established business. These services primarily offer advice and counselling for small firm entrepreneurs and might suggest financing options, but finding Business Angel finance is usually not their principal activity.

Company Literature

Business Link is a nationwide network of around 230 advice centres. It provides affordable advice to all small and medium-sized businesses, especially those with a potential to grow.

Each Business Link has two core services, the Business Information Service and Business Advice.

Business Information Service

The information service provides a single, local point of access for all business information and advice. This ranges from services delivered by TECs and Enterprise agencies to those provided by private organisations such as marketing consultancies and accountants.

Previously, companies wanting business services in their area had to wade through a diverse number of channels. These sometimes overlapped, were often hard to find and almost always confusing. In the case of export advice, for example, a company would have had to decide whether to approach the local government office, the Chamber of Commerce, the TEC, or a private consultancy specialising in the field. Now they can simply contact the local Business Link which will either answer the query itself or bring in the relevant organisation.

Business Advice

The second main platform of the service is tailored, on-the-spot advice from a range of specialist advisers. At the heart of the service is the personal business adviser (PBA) who provides independent, affordable and long-term help, if necessary, over several years. This fulfils a fundamental gap in the market. Although there is plenty of short-term help available for small businesses, most companies need sustained support over a period of time in order to achieve significant change.

PBAs will help companies write a business strategy and implement it. In the process, they help overcome many of the classic cultural, organisational and financial barriers to growth. These range from a lack of strategic planning because management is too busy firefighting daily operational pressures, to the need to create a management structure, motivate staff, control cashflow or benchmark against competitors.

The PBA also acts as the channel through which other expert resources from the Business Link can be accessed. When required, the PBA will bring in expert advisers from five key areas: export, finance, innovation and technology, design, and training. These advisers help with everything from finding innovative sources of finance to new product development.

Cost

Pricing structures vary between Business Links but the fundamental premise is that they should be accessible and affordable. Typically, a PBA might undertake an initial business review free of charge and then provide subsidised ongoing consultancy.

Structure

All Business Links are private sector organisations comprising a number of partners. Partners typically include TECs, Chambers of Commerce, Local Authorities, Enterprise Agencies, universities, banks and others. Each Business Link's board of directors will draw on partner organisations and local businesses.

Business Link Signpost Line

Companies wanting to be directed to their nearest Business Link should call the Business Link Signpost Line on 0345 567765.

Financial Advisers

Financial Advisers are one of the key services provided by all Business Links. They help businesses with everything from financial management systems, including cashflow and forecasts, to business plans and finding an appropriate accountant.

Financial advisers also help find innovative sources of finance ranging from Business Angels, factoring and grants to "soft loans" such as the various loan guarantee schemes. The aim is to get businesses to think more imaginatively and not just rely on bank loans. The service meets an important need identified in independent research. Although large companies have access to numerous sources of advice, such as the corporate finance departments of large accountancy firms, there is little provision for small firms that is totally independent and which they can afford.

Business Angels

All Business Links have access to Business Angel programmes, which act as a matchmaking service between potential investors and businesses with growth potential that need finance and management expertise in specific areas. The local Business Link may have a database of private investors in the region prepared to act as Business Angels. These local registers usually comprise 60 or 70 investors, while national registers may have over 600.

The average investment is £50 000, with a timescale of about five years and a potential return on investment of 10–20 per cent.

Cambridge Venture Management Ltd

Charlie Brown
Cambridge Venture Management Ltd
Richmond House
16–20 Regent Street
Cambridge CB2 1DB

Tel.: 01223 302305
Fax: 01223 302307

Date of formation: 1984
Organisation type: Private—Interim
  management service
Geographical area: UK and US
Matching methods: Render active
  managerial input to firms seeking finance
Industry preferences: All
Stage of investment: All
Additional services: Render expertise to
  investee

Authors' Summary

Cambridge Venture Management team members become actively involved in the managerial activities of the firms they are assisting in the procurement of outside finance. This is primarily a consulting service to entrepreneurial companies.

Company Literature

Cambridge Venture Management Limited (CVM) assists entrepreneurs and companies to devise and implement business development strategies. It also works with clients to raise finance from private investors and venture capital funds, as well as guiding negotiations with existing shareholders and banks, where changes in capital structure are required.

Much of CVM's ability to add value to client business derives from its extensive networks and its knowledge of private investors, management and investing institutions. In co-operation with its partners MNS Cambridge International, based in San Diego and Boston, USA, CVM also helps European businesses set up operations in the USA, and provides assistance to US companies seeking partners and market entry strategies in the UK and Europe.

The directors of the company are all based in Cambridge, UK. Other members of the board have wide-ranging experience of international and merchant banking, management consultancy and venture capital investments.

Capital Access

Melanie Perkins
Capital Access
GMBIC Ltd
Windmill Lane
Denton
Greater Manchester M34 3QS

Tel.: 0161 337 8648
Fax: 0161 337 8651
Email: gmbic@attmail.com

Date of formation: 1993
Organisation type: Economic Development
  Agency
Geographical area: Cheshire/Manchester
Matching methods: Investor newsletter
Investment £ sought: £10 000–£250 000
No. of investors: 35
Successful matches (July 1995–June 1996):
  3
Industry preferences: All
Stage of investment: Development,
  expansion and acquisition
Additional services: full range of services

Authors' Summary

Supported by the local chamber of commerce, Capital Access attempts to match small entrepreneurial firms (usually in their early stages) with local Business Angels seeking involvement in such ventures. A short summary of the investment proposal is sent to a group of subscribers, who can contact the entrepreneurs directly.

Company Literature

Capital Access provides a way for businesses in the Greater Manchester area with growth potential to raise capital funding in the range of £10 000–£250 000. The scheme is designed to fill the gap where bank finance may not be appropriate or the amount sought is less than established venture capital funders will consider. It may be the answer for established businesses, or start-ups, which require capital to: fund growth, support new products, processes and develop opportunities, or make an acquisition.

Capital is provided directly by private investors, who want to invest personal funds in exchange for a share of a business. In addition, most investors are also keen to offer their own management expertise. If certain criteria are met, investors may be able to qualify for tax relief on their investment.

Through Capital Access, profitable partnerships are established, bringing together businesses requiring equity funding and people with an entrepreneurial flair seeking investment opportunities. Capital Access is a personalised, cost-effective route to capital investment opportunities.

If you have either an existing business or a commercially viable business idea, which you believe offers growth potential, then Capital Access can help you raise the funding required. You will need to be able to convince potential investors that you have an available business plan based on realistic assumptions and that you can achieve your objectives within a reasonable timeframe. The scheme can then provide your growing business with the right partner from a range of investors, who have cash to inject as well as experience and expertise to offer.

If we decide your proposal could meet investors' criteria the next stage would be to formulate a two-page summary of your business plan. This will be agreed with you prior to circulation to interested investors. Usually, we would ask you to make a short presentation on your proposals to a group of potential investors. The next step would be for investors expressing an interest to receive a full copy of your business plan before arranging to meet you.

We continue to provide support and guidance during the negotiation process with private investors.

Capital Connections

Michael Thompson/Philip Dobson
Capital Connections
ELTEC Ltd
Red Rose Court
Clayton Business Park
Clayton-le-Moors
Accrington BB5 5JR

Tel.: 01254 301333
Fax: 01254 399090

Date of formation: 1992
Organisation type: TEC
Geographical area: North-West UK
Matching methods: investor newsletter
Investment £ sought: £5000–£300 000
No. of investors: 43
Successful matches (July 1995–June 1996): 2
Industry preferences: All
Stage of investment: All
Additional services: Advice and business plan formulation

Authors' Summary

Capital Connections attempt to match entrepreneurial firms and Business Angel subscribers based on the investment preferences and/or through distribution of investment summaries to potential investors. This service operates locally in the Lancashire area.

Company Literature

Capital Connections is an introductory service set up by ELTEC in 1992 with the purpose of helping small and medium-sized enterprises raise capital by putting them in touch with potential investors. It was one of the five pilot schemes initially supported by the Department of Trade and Industry to foster informal investment in new and growing businesses.

While primarily aimed at furthering the development of business and employment in the North-West and, in particular, East Lancashire the scheme will, nevertheless, consider applications for help from other parts of the country. Some 45 per cent of the growing number of potential investors registered with Capital Connections are based outside its main operating region.

Entrepreneurial companies seeking finance are required to complete a company profile form and submit a business plan. This is followed up with a meeting with one of the named contacts. Potential investors are also required to complete a profile form, indicating their investment preferences and management skills. Capital Connections then attempts to match the one to the other and effect an introduction. This may be through a review of the database using specific matching criteria, or in response to a coded synopsis of the business project being distributed to a range of potential investors registered with the scheme. Unless and until matters progress to a formal introduction, the two parties remain anonymous and at all times strict confidentiality is maintained.

Once an introduction has taken place, Capital Connections plays no further part and the two sides are left to carry out their own due diligence enquiries and negotiate their own agreements in consultation with their respective professional advisers.

ELTEC itself is able to provide a range of services to new and growing companies within Lancashire, including help in preparing their business plans. While a charge may be made for these services, neither the companies seeking funds nor the potential investors are, at present, charged for being registered with Capital Connections and no success fees are levied.

The Capital Market

Jeff Newall
The Capital Market
c/o Business Link Milton Keynes
   & North Bucks
Tempus
249 Midsummer Boulevard
Central Milton Keynes
Buckinghamshire MK9 1EU

Tel.: 01908 660004
Fax: 01908 230130

Date of formation: 1994
Organisation type: Business Link
Geographical area: Milton Keynes and
   north Buckinghamshire, Bedfordshire
Matching methods: Investment bulletin
   circulated and presentations
Investment £ sought: £10 000–£500 000
No. of investors: 118
Successful matches (July 1995–June 1996):
   11
Industry preferences: All
Stage of investment: All
Additional services: Workshops and
   seminars

Authors' Summary

The Capital Market aims to match unquoted companies with potential investors. It does this through circulating company profiles to likely investors and organising investor presentations for those companies that have induced some interest. This service is primarily intended for those companies, investors and intermediaries in the Milton Keynes, North Bucks or Bedfordshire areas.

Company Literature

The Capital Market is an informal investment scheme which helps unquoted companies at any stage of development, and in any industry, find investors willing to make equity investments. Many of the registered investors have business skills that can be used to assist companies to grow and develop.

Clients

Companies who wish to use the service should be located or willing to locate in Milton Keynes, North Bucks or Bedfordshire and be willing to at least consider selling equity. They should also present a business plan. Investors eligible for the service should be seeking investment opportunities of £10 000–£500 000 and may have business experience which could prove of value to the investee company.

   Intermediaries who in their professional capacity work with clients can also benefit from the opportunities presented by The Capital Market.

How does The Capital Market Help Companies?

- Initial discussion—Capital Market welcomes calls from companies seeking £10 000–£500 000.
- One-hour meeting—if a company seems appropriate, its entrepreneurs will be invited to a meeting to discuss it in more detail.
- Two page summary—after registering with the service, the company will be advised on how to draw up a two-page summary, which will be circulated to investors Capital Market believes might be interested.

- Direct contact—if interest is shown, Capital Market will contact the company and arrange for them to contact the potential investor directly.
- One-paragraph description—a single paragraph description will be added to Capital Market's anonymous list and circulated to all investors of the service.
- Investment fairs and presentations—some companies will be asked to make a 15-minute investor presentation.

How does The Capital Market Help Investors?

- Telephone/questionnaire—information is collected on the investor's investment criteria.
- One paragraph descriptions—with the investor's registration form, he/she receives a current list of investment opportunities, each described in a single paragraph. Should the investor formally register, updated lists will be sent regularly.
- Summaries—two-page summaries will be sent to the investor of those opportunities of particular interest, subject to the company's agreement.
- Direct contact—if an investor has an investment opportunity of particular interest, Capital Market will contact the company and arrange for them to call the investor. Capital Market will then stand back from discussions but remain in touch with both parties to monitor progress.

Capital Match

Howard Matthews/Susan Nunn
Capital Match
Suite G
The King Business Centre
Reeds Lane
Sayers Common
Hassocks
West Sussex BN6 9LS

Tel.: 01273 833881
Fax: 01273 833277

Date of formation: 1994
Organisation type: Business Link
Geographical area: Hampshire, Surrey,
Sussex and Isle of Wight
Matching methods: Personal and computer
Investment £ sought: £30 000+
No. of investors: 32
Successful matches (July 1995–June 1996):
4
Industry preferences: All
Stage of investment: All
Additional services: Investor club and
seminars/workshops

Authors' Summary

Capital Match is a local business introduction service dedicated to matching entrepreneurs and potential investors in Sussex, Surrey, Hampshire and the Isle of Wight. Capital Match utilises computer and personal matching and offers Investor Club meetings and seminars and workshops to businesses and entrepreneurs.

Company Literature

Capital Match's main objective is to bring together the equity finance needs of small and medium-sized businesses (needing £20 000+) with investors willing to commit time, energy and capital to suitable investment opportunities.

As part of the government's central initiative to support small and medium-sized businesses, county Business Links (under the umbrella of Training and Enterprise Councils) have endeavoured to provide a "one stop" service providing comprehensive information and advice.

The provision of equity funding through the medium of individual private investment, however, requires specialist knowledge of share and deal structures. It was therefore agreed jointly between the Business Links of Sussex, Surrey and Hampshire to subcontract the management administration of a Business Angel scheme, "Capital Match", to The Cadmus Organisation Limited, an established corporate finance business that was already managing the local area Midland Enterprise Fund.

Capital Match commenced operations in 1994 and was joined by the Isle of Wight Business Link in January 1997. Annual fees for businesses, private investors and advisers alike, at the time of writing is £250 plus VAT. An additional success fee of £1000 plus 2.5 per cent of sum raised is payable to Capital Match.

Who is it For?

- Private investors—private individuals who can demonstrate the availability of cash with the option to bring their expertise to a business.
- Businesses—based in Sussex, Surrey, Hampshire and the Isle of Wight.
- Advisers—with client companies looking for money or individuals looking for investment opportunities.

How Does it Work?

Complete and return an application form. Investors will be invited for an interview where investment criteria will be discussed in detail; they are given a copy of the investor directory and registered business summary, and can attend all events at no extra cost throughout the year.

Businesses will be visited in order to review the business plan and identify key features of the business. A company profile is then written and circulated to all registered investors and advisers. The business will have the opportunity to present its proposal to a meeting of registered investors.

Advisers are sent company profiles throughout their year of registration; they are offered a percentage of the completion fee following a successful investment in respect of any company recommended to Capital Match, and can attend appropriate events and bring clients.

Cavendish Management Resources (CMR)

Michael Downey/Peter Dodds
Cavendish Management Resources
13 Harley Street
London W1N 1DA

Date of formation: 1984
Organisation type: Private—corporate
finance
Geographical area: UK
Matching methods: Personal matching
Investment £ sought: None
No. of investors: 200+
Successful matches (July 1995–June 1996):
11
Industry preferences: All (not property)
Stage of investment: All
Additional services: Intellectual property

Tel.: 0171 636 1744
Fax: 0171 637 2600

protection, licensing, consultancy,
mergers and acquisitions

Authors' Summary

Cavendish Management Resources (CMR) utilises its database of potential investors to find financial backing for unquoted businesses seeking funding. If a match is probable, CMR will assist with the negotiations and will also provide additional management support where needed. CMR's executives are available for both short and long-term assignments as appropriate.

Company Literature

CMR combines the financial resources of several hundred private investors with the skills and expertise of a network of experienced executives. CMR's investors are constantly seeking good business propositions. CMR's executives work closely with client companies to ensure that funding can be obtained quickly and professionally.

Where CMR believes that changes may be necessary to attract investment, this will be discussed with the client. There is no charge for this preliminary assessment.

When CMR is satisfied that the proposition can attract investment, the client company will be introduced to its investors for direct discussions. CMR will assist in those negotiations to help find the formula that is right for both parties. The investment agreement will be between the investor and the company, both of whom should take their own independent professional advice before completing.

In addition to its investor base of several hundred private investors, CMR also has a similar number of senior executives. This combination of wide-ranging executive expertise and private investment fund provides an exceptional support base for small to medium-sized businesses.

CMR's executives are all senior managers with many years of experience of business at the sharp end. Most have held board appointments in major corporations, but now exercise their professional skills for the benefit of smaller companies. The diversity of industries and disciplines in which these executives have expertise, enables CMR to provide specialist support to companies in every market sector.

A fundamental aspect of CMR's policy is to commit fully to achieving success for its clients. To this end, CMR will usually defer part of its remuneration on to a performance-related basis. As a result, CMR's involvement is never a major issue financially, with much reward being derived from increased profitability of value.

With its investor base providing access to over £200 million of funds for its clients, and with a broad skill base of executive expertise, CMR is dedicated to helping small to medium-sized businesses expand and grow profitably.

Cheshire Contacts

Pauline Randles
Cheshire County Council
Economic Development Service
4 Hillards Court
Chester Business Park
Wrexham Road
Chester CH4 9RD

Tel.: 01244 603152
Fax: 01244 603003

Date of formation: 1994
Organisation type: Local Authority
Geographical area: UK, primarily Cheshire
Matching methods: Newsletter
Investment £ sought: £5000–£500 000
No. of investors: 19
Successful matches (July 1995–June 1996):
   n/a
Industry preferences: All
Stage of investment: All

Authors' Summary

As a non-profit service, Cheshire Contacts distributes a free investment opportunity magazine to potential investors in the geographical area. All matching is done on a confidential basis. For a small fee, companies in Cheshire can be featured in the magazine, while both the magazine subscription and a response to an investment opportunity are free for potential investors.

Company Literature

Cheshire Contacts is a free quarterly magazine, designed to promote investment in Cheshire and to enable companies and individuals to identify business contacts, which are sometimes difficult to make through normal channels. The magazine is distributed to entrepreneurs, private, company and institutional investors, such as venture capitalists, merchant banks and senior industry executives.

On average, companies looking for investment and advertising in *Cheshire Contacts* are introduced to three potential partners. By means of a box number, investors are put in touch with their particular investment preferences, providing opportunity of shorter or long-term investment.

To be included, companies have to be based in Cheshire and must pay an advertising fee of £25 plus VAT for a 60-word summary in *Cheshire Contacts*. The service advises advertisers in the "Investment Contact" section to note the requirements of the Financial Services Act and to seek guidance from an accountant or solicitor. For investors responding to an advertisement, the Cheshire Contacts service is free.

Cheshire Contact's introduction service between investors and investment opportunities in Cheshire is fully confidential and aims to provide an invaluable link between individuals and company investors seeking additional investment and/or expertise.

Corbett Keeling Ltd

Jim Keeling
Corbett Keeling Limited
20 St Swithin's Lane
London EC4N 8AD

Tel.: 0171 626 6266
Fax: 0171 626 7005

Date of formation: Spring 1997
Organisation type: Private
Geographical area: UK
Matching methods: Full investment adviser
Investment £ sought: £10 000–£1 million
  (per investor)
No. of subscribers: n/a
Successful matches (July 1995–June 1996):
  n/a
Industry preferences: All
Stage of investment: Established/expansion
Additional services: Full range

Authors' Summary

Corbett Keeling is usually retained by the owners of the business requiring finance, and it manages the whole process of raising finance. Corbett Keeling presents prospective deals to investors, and specialises in raising funds for firms making, or which will shortly make, £500 000 profit and which require over £500 000 finance.

Company Literature

Corbett Keeling specialises in advising UK private businesses on raising equity finance. Finance is raised from institutional sources and private individuals.

Institutional sources range from traditional venture capitalists to niche institutions that are not so widely known for making investments in private companies.

Private investors range from those able to make single investments in excess of £1 million to groups who would invest in amounts of less than £10 000 each.

Funds are raised from the most suitable source for the business requiring them. This may be a single institution or a syndicate of institutions, one private investor, a small group of private investors, a mixed group of investors with the shares quoted on OFEX, a widely marketed scheme with tax incentives such as Enterprise Investment Scheme or Reinvestment Relief, or the most suitable mix of the above.

Features of a Corbett Keeling Financing

Corbett Keeling is generally retained by the owners of the business requiring finance. It manages the whole process of raising finance including advising on the amount to be raised, designing the best deal structure, writing investment circulars, co-ordinating other professional advisers and sourcing the most suitable form of equity.

Corbett Keeling presents prospective deals to investors in a form that makes investing as simple as possible. Equity provided may be new to fund expansion or replacement to enable existing shareholders to sell shares. Deals are structured to take advantage of relevant tax reliefs for investors and owners of investee businesses alike.

Corbett Keeling focuses on businesses making, or which will shortly make, £500 000 profit and which require over £500 000 finance.

Daily Telegraph Business Network

Gavin Wetton
Daily Telegraph Business Network
1 Canada Square
Canary Wharf
London E14 5AT

Date of formation: 1992
Organisation type: Investment publisher
Geographical area: UK and worldwide
Matching methods: Investment bulletins
Investment £ sought: All
No. of investors: n/a
Successful matches (July 1995–June 1996): n/a
Industry preferences: All
Stage of investment: All

Tel.: 0171 538 7172
Fax: 0171 538 7155

Additional services: Other business-related sections published

Authors' Summary

Small to medium-sized firms seeking finance and management input may advertise their needs in The Daily Telegraph Network. This service distributes a summary of all information in the *Daily Telegraph* and a more detailed subscription in a bulletin to which interested investors must subscribe.

Company Literature

The Daily Telegraph Business Network, founded in January 1992, was created to offer a specialist marketing platform for the small to medium-sized business enterprise, to alert the business world of its specific requirements.

With a readership of 2.7 million—of whom 204 000 are business people—the *Daily Telegraph*'s high profile and unbiased position allows it to provide a unique introduction service.

The value of this service is now recognised by both the business person and the Business Angel. Each group has its own interests, whether it be to expand, divest, sell or seek investors/investment. The Network provides the ideal platform for approaching private investors, acquisitive businesses, overseas or national companies seeking strategic alliances and those wishing to sell, quite possibly prior to retirement.

The network does not charge a "success fee", therefore there is no financial incentive to follow up introductions effected through the service; however, news of successful introductions, completed transactions and letters from satisfied Business Network customers are received regularly.

A major benefit of using the Daily Telegraph Business Network is the fact that your investment opportunity does not "die" on the day, it goes on to our database where it stays for up to 12 months. Since there is a charge made to those wishing to obtain information, the placer is protected from "timewasters".

Dunstable Management Group

Oliver Diggle
Dunstable Management Group
PO Box 18
Dereham
Norfolk NR20 4UL

Tel.: 01362 637948
Fax: 01362 637581

Date of formation: 1992
Organisation type: Private—interim
  management service
Geographical area: UK
Matching methods: Personal and computer
Investment £ sought: £25 000–£1 million
No. of investors: 180
Successful matches (July 1995–June 1996):
  3
Industry preferences: All
Stage of investment: Expansions, start-up if
  entrepreneur has experience/track record
Additional services: Management support
  consultancy, interim management

Authors' Summary

Dunstable Management Group (DMG) is an interim management service which works closely with small to medium-sized companies to advise them on how best to obtain finance. A personal client approach and a computer database are utilised in the matching process.

Company Literature

The DMG is a working association of independent and senior professionals specialising in advising on fund-raising issues and the provision of related management and advisory services by working closely with managing directors, business proprietors and prospective owners of small to medium-sized companies.

The group starts its work where a business recognises the need to address a funding issue whether for: refinancing, reconstruction or restructuring existing debt, corporate expansion programmes, asset finance, mergers and acquisitions, MBOs and MBIs, and some start-ups.

In working alongside chief executive clients, members of the group assist in:

- assessing the feasibility of raising finance
- raising funds for corporate ventures
- assessing and advising on business plans, which may involve some further business and market analysis
- structuring financial packages and financial engineering
- approaching and negotiating with sources of finance, which may include Business Angels
- grants, trade investors, institutions or an outright purchase, of the business
- supporting negotiations until agreement has been reached
- acting, where required, as an independent director or introducing to the client a suitably qualified and experienced one.

Each enquiry is different, and DMG will first assess the feasibility of raising finance, usually by a visit to the company. If it appears feasible, a plan of action including a quotation for costs will be prepared.

DMG keeps a register of Business Angels known to it, and works with other Angel networks and consultancies where this form of finance is appropriate.

The Enterprise Forum

John Wilson
The Enterprise Forum
19 Gardyn Croft
Taverham
Norwich NR8 6UZ

Date of formation: 1995
Organisation type: Private
Geographical area: Norfolk and Suffolk
Matching methods: Presentations at
meetings
Investment £ sought: All
No. of investors: 47
Successful matches (July 1995–June 1996):
4

Tel.: 01603 260576
Fax: 01603 260576

Industry preferences: All
Stage of investment: All

Authors' Summary

The Enterprise Forum hold investment meetings with entrepreneurs and potential investors. These are held when demand dictates and are usually informal affairs. The Forum's main purpose is to instigate the introduction, not to act as a business adviser.

Company Literature

The Enterprise Forum is managed by LaLance via the principals, David Herman and John Wilson. LaLance is a foundation in accordance with Dutch law and its management of The Forum reflects its Anglo/Dutch connections. Its activities are aimed primarily at developing businesses within Norfolk and Suffolk.

The Forum maintains a list of approximately 80 individuals who have either expressed an interest in investing in start-up or developing companies or who are professional representatives of such individuals. The Forum is, as its name suggests, a meeting held when the need arises. That need is indicated by firms wishing to raise capital signifying to LaLance that they are prepared to make personal presentations at the Forum meeting.

Presenting firms are encouraged to have a business plan to hand out, but for the purposes of the meeting, product demonstrations and the personalities of the presenters are considered as being substantially important.

The meetings are normally at breakfast time and may, from time to time, include guest speakers to talk on subjects of general economic or financial significance.

The Forum requires no formal membership qualification or annual fee for attendance on the part of potential investors or their advisers. A modest contribution to the costs of each meeting is made.

Presenting firms are charged a non-refundable commitment fee of £200 and, should funds be raised, an additional fee of 3 per cent of the sum raised on the first £100 000 (with a minimum fee of £1000) and 1 per cent on any excess thereover. Presenting firms are also offered the opportunity to access national investor networks on a cost covering basis.

Neither The Forum nor LaLance offer financial advice to firms presenting as part of the standard arrangements. Potential investors are urged to ensure that due diligence is undertaken by their own professional advisers.

The Forum operates an open co-operation policy with other introduction services and LaLance is a member and supporter of the Private Equity Funding Association (PEFA).

Entrust

Bob Marris
Entrust
Portman House
Portland Road
Newcastle upon Tyne NE2 1AQ

Tel.: 0191 261 4838
Fax: 0191 261 4108

E-mail: enquire@entrust.co.uk

Date of formation: 1982
Organisation type: Enterprise Agency
Geographical area: North-East
Matching methods: Database, investment
   meetings and bulletins
Investment £ sought: £10 000+
No. of investors: 94
Successful matches (July 1995–June 1996):
   6
Industry preferences: All
Stage of investment: All
Additional services: Training and
   counselling

Authors' Summary

Entrust is a business introduction service which concentrates primarily on the north east. It uses database matching, investment presentations and a bulletin to match entrepreneurs and investors. Entrust also offers counselling on the most appropriate ways to obtain the finance the entrepreneurial firm is seeking.

Company Literature

Entrust was formed in 1982 and is one of the largest Enterprise Agencies in the country. As such it delivers into the Tyne and Wear area a wide range of training, counselling support programmes and consultancy.

Investor Forum (IF)

In June 1984 the private equity matching commenced. This service operates primarily in the north-east, delivering service to the Business Links of Durham, Northumberland, Sunderland, Teesside and Tyneside. Any deal size and any sector specialisation will be accepted for matching consideration, only the quality of the proposal must be confirmed before further progression.

Procedures

All investees undergo a strenuous vetting procedure to establish suitability for the programme.

If acceptable, a professionally produced business plan has to support the requirements. Advice is given on how best to structure the financial package and assistance will be given on sourcing the most appropriate forms of finance including grants.

Start-ups, MBOs, MBIs, expansion and acquisition proposals will be given assistance.

An anonymous synopsis of the business plan consisting of approximately 250 words is circulated to our database. Investees also have the opportunity to make presentations to potential investors.

Our investors include some of the most successful business people in the region and some are prepared to pool resources and form a consortia.

EquityLink

Bernard Hallewell
Business Link Hertfordshire
45 Grosvenor Road
St Albans
Hertfordshire AL1 3AW

Tel.: 01727 813533
Fax: 01727 813442

Date of formation: 1994
Organisation type: Business Link
Geographical area: Hertfordshire
Matching methods: Confidential personal
  matching service
Investment £ sought: £50 000–£250 000
No. of investors: 76
Successful matches (July 1995–June 1996):
  12
Industry preferences: All
Stage of investment: All
Additional services: Business plan
  counselling

Authors' Summary

EquityLink aims to assist small to medium-sized firms in acquiring Business Angel finance to expand and grow. This Business Link also offers additional services to assist entrepreneurs in the financial management, business plan presentation, and guidance of their firms.

Company Literature

EquityLink™ was launched in October 1994 to provide a flexible, confidential Business Angel network to Hertfordshire companies. It works with existing companies with growth attributes seeking expansion capital. As of January 1997, some 25 companies have successfully attracted equity through the service and raised some £4.29 million.

EquityLink™ receives referrals from bankers, accountants and solicitors, working in collaboration rather than in reaction. It also has established a network of investors to whom deal information could quickly and informally be circulated. Over 130 potential investors have registered and around 60 are considered to be actively seeking deals at any one time.

The service is firmly based on the confidentiality of the process and the methods of introduction employed. It seeks to bring the individual parties into contact as soon as possible so that a relationship between potential partners has the greatest possible time in which to develop. Its investor event format underpins this process.

In order for a firm seeking finance to gain access to the Business Angel investors, it has to pass a rigorous process of selection. This involves meeting with a Business Link manager initially, and then drawing up a strong and viable business plan for submission to the potential investor network. The staff at EquityLink™ have the expertise to assist the entrepreneur through this process.

The typical firm seeking finance will be established—that is, it will have been trading profitably for at least 10 months—and will be at that critical stage where growth is not just essential, but can be confidently projected.

Companies beyond Hertfordshire are eligible to be considered for EquityLink™ either through one of its associated schemes or direct. However, published tariffs apply only to Hertfordshire-based companies or clients.

EquityLink™ is a service provided by Business Link Hertfordshire and forms part of its integrated Financial Packaging Service.

EquityLink (Kent)

Peter Kitching
Finance Development Manager
Business Link Kent
26 Kings Hill Avenue
Kings Hill
West Malling
Kent ME19 4TA

Tel.: 01732 878000
Fax: 01732 874818

Date of formation: 1994
Organisation type: Business Link
Geographical area: Kent
Matching methods: Confidential matching
Investment £ sought: £50 000–£250 000
No. of investors: 70
Successful matches (July 1995–June 1996):
4
Industry preferences: All
Stage of investment: All
Additional services: Business plan
counselling

Authors' Summary

EquityLink (Kent) seeks to match companies looking for £10 000+ in funding with investors who have at least £20 000 to invest. These matches are done through personal introductions in the strictest confidence. EquityLink (Kent) also has business advisers who conduct business plan reviews for those firms seeking finance.

Company Literature

EquityLink (Kent) has been set up to facilitate the matching of individuals or private companies seeking to invest in new and ongoing businesses based in Kent, requiring equity or near equity funds to meet growth or start-up aspirations and plans.

To date EquityLink has in excess of 70 potential investors who have indicated that they have funds available for investment.

Their basic procedure is that all those seeking funds are required to register with EquityLink by completing a form, as well as providing EquityLink with a business plan and a synopsis of the project. Following receipt of a project, one of EquityLink's business advisers visits the applicant and talks through the detail of the plan. The business adviser will also test its completeness, internal consistency and financial robustness.

The business adviser will provide guidance as to what investors are looking for in a business plan. Once the business plan has been scrutinised, a synopsis of the plan is circulated to investors. If there are a number of investors interested in the project, EquityLink arranges a presentation by the applicant. However, if only one or two investors express interest, EquityLink puts the two parties in direct contact.

EquityLink also arranges an informal initial meeting between investee company and investor prior to submission of the business plan to see if they are compatible and have a chemistry that will work in a business partnership.

Investment fairs are held on a regular basis with 10 investee companies taking a stand where they can introduce themselves to a number of investors on an informal basis.

To be included, companies must be looking for £10 000+ and investors must have £20 000 to invest. The two will then be matched by EquityLink through a personal introduction in the strictest confidence.

Great Eastern Investment Forum

Nigel Brown/Jo Caley
Great Eastern Investment Forum
Richmond House
16–20 Regent Street
Cambridge CB2 1DB

Tel.: 01223 357131
Fax: 01223 353705

Date of formation: 1995
Organisation type: Private—organiser of
  investment meetings/forums
Geographical area: East Anglia
Matching methods: Investment
  presentations to potential investors
Investment £ sought: £25 000–£1 million
No. of investors: 205
Successful matches (July 1995–June 1996):
  9
Industry preferences: All
Stage of investment: All
Additional services: Newsletter, breakfast
  meetings, presentation advice

Authors' Summary

The Great Eastern Investment Forum holds breakfast meetings (every two months) and distributes a newsletter as a means of providing Business Angels with a selection of entrepreneurial investment opportunities primarily based in the East Anglia area.

Company Literature

Designed to support the growth in risk capital projects in the small and medium-sized firms sector, the Great Eastern Investment Forum has raised £1.3 million in its first year, for a total of eight start-up or developing enterprises.

Classless

The aim, according to Forum Chairman, Nigel Brown, is to create a classless venture capital market: "We are creating an environment where businesses of any size can declare an interest in venture capital as a means of funding new plant or growing existing ones. Smaller businesses, or those requiring small sums should not feel left out as there are plenty of opportunities."

Interest from both investors and young companies across East Anglia, London and the South-East has been gathering momentum in recent months and the Forum is extremely bullish about the prospects of a real funding boost for expanding businesses in those areas.

The Forum is attracting over a hundred people (as an average) to breakfast meetings, which are held every two months, in different locations. The number and mix of attendees reflect the broad base of the area's economy at professional adviser, investor and entrepreneur levels. Hi-tech, research and development, agriculture, manufacturing, retail and service sector—all key sectors—are consistently supporting Forum events.

Instrumental

This profile has been instrumental in bringing together the central characters to the "plot". In its role as a dating agency, the Forum has established biannual presentations, where companies seeking funding have the chance to set out their case to potential investors.

This formula has also been successful in drawing on the potential investor base of over 250 private and institutional Forum members. From these presentations, lasting relationships have been established.

Confidence

The main role of the Forum is to establish dialogue with firms of this size and introduce them to sources of funding. However, because small firms tend to need more support in the early years, the Forum is keen to see investors taking a broader interest in the companies they help to fund, where this is appropriate.

In practice, this means that investors can also put themselves forward to companies as consultants, non-executive directors, or just offering the broad shoulders of a Business Angel. A combination of funding and advice or support is seen, by the Forum, as an important mix for start-ups in particular.

Halo Ltd

Jeff Skinner
Halo Ltd
8 Sorrell Court
Highcliffe
Christchurch
Dorset BH23 4XY

Tel.: 01425 272945
Fax: 01425 272945

Date of formation: 1994
Organisation type: Private
Geographical area: London and the South
Matching methods: Personal criteria
matching, investment bulletins and
presentations
Investment £ sought: £50 000–£10 million
No. of subscribers: 98
Successful matches (July 1995–June 1996):
5
Industry preferences: All
Stage of investment: All, especially
expansion, MBO, MBI (few start-up)
Additional services: Management
consultancy services

Authors' Summary

Halo is a business introduction service which specialises in seeking finance for small established firms (£50 000–£10 million) that want to expand and often also need management expertise to support the existing team. Halo does not do start-up financing. It also offers firms seeking capital a full range of services to aid the search for finance (i.e. creation of business plan, business summaries, etc.). Halo tends to specialise geographically in the southern counties.

Company Literature

Halo is a private Business Angel network and management consultancy service that covers most of the southern counties for businesses and investors who prefer the benefits of a personal, professional, confidential working relationship. Recent restructuring of its service now enables Halo Ltd to provide introductions for its clients to a range of services from professional advisers to cover MBOs, MBIs, flotations, investment agreements, due diligence, patents, intellectual property, tax issues, corporate lawyers, accountants, etc.

Services to Business

Halo's service for businesses is primarily for established companies who are considering expansion that requires new investment (typically £50 000–£10 million) and management expertise to support the existing team. Importantly, full support with creation of the business plan, business summaries and group presentations is available from the beginning of their search for finance. Halo can also supply access to on-going post-investment consultancy covering business development, marketing, merchandising, IT solutions, and human resource management.

Registration fees for business are from £350 plus a reducing success fee from 5 per cent. Fees for consultancy support are negotiated around specific individual requirements.

Inclusion criteria—must have a viable business opportunity with good growth potential backed by sound management with equity available.

Service to Investors

For investors Halo provides confidential access to a wide variety of business opportunities, supported by targeted circulation of individual summaries and a general newsletter with additional access to investment forums and educational seminars.

Registration fees for investors are £125 per annum with additional modest fees for attendance at specific seminars.

Introduction Methods

One hundred per cent personal against stated criteria from the investor and investee. Circulation of individual summaries and newsletter. Investor forums.

Other Information

Halo has an average 30 opportunities available with a network of private investors of around 90 from across the southern counties. Last year it successfully introduced around £1 million to businesses seeking finance.

Hilling Wall Corporate Finance

Chris Hilling/Andrew Wall/Richard
  Bowes
Hilling Wall Corporate Finance
43 South Street
Mayfair
London W1Y 5PD

Tel.: 0171 495 1302
Fax: 0171 495 1303

E-mail: hilling-wall@avnet.co.uk
Web site: www.avnet.co.uk/hw

Date of formation: 1989
Organisation type: Private—corporate
  finance
Geographical area: UK
Matching methods: Informal networking
  contacts and matching services
Investment £ sought: £150 000–£10 million
No. of investors: 50
Successful matches (July 1995–June 1996):
  7
Industry preferences: All (but retail/
  property)
Stage of investment: All (prefer established)
Additional services: Provide financial,
  investment and taxation advice

Authors' Summary

In addition to offering an array of finance related services, Hilling Wall Corporate Finance also aims to raise capital for unquoted firms from private investors. This is done through informal networking contacts and in-house matching. Hilling Wall prefers to assist firms that need funding in the region of £150 000–£10 million.

Company Literature

Hilling Wall Corporate Finance partners and advisers are specialists in corporate advisory services, investigations, tax, valuations and other skills required to provide our clients with a comprehensive service.

The partners and advisers have a background in merchant banking and personal taxation, due diligence, venture capital and industry. The overall philosophy is to strictly limit the number of engagements we will handle at any time commensurate with our time and resources available, and we do not delegate our responsibility to junior or inexperienced staff.

Services Provided

- Capital raising and finance
- Management buy-outs and buy-ins
- Acquisition searches and negotiations and disposals
- Investigations and due diligence
- Short and long form reporting accountants
- Valuations
- Taxation advice

Capital Raising and Finance

Identifying and introducing the right type of investor, whether a venture capitalist, private investor or another source of funds, is one of the most critical stages in successfully financing any project or company.

For larger investments, Hilling Wall has considerable experience in the market and can demonstrate this through its track record. For those interested in this service, an annual guide, *A Selective Review of Venture Capital Companies*, is published and is available on request.

Most recently Hilling Wall has acted as financial adviser to an OFEX admission, and as reporting accountant to a stock exchange transaction and an OFEX fund-raising.

Acquisitions and Disposals

Hilling Wall regularly identifies and negotiates transactions. It manages the project from opening discussion and liaison with company accountants and other advisers, through to completion with the related taxation affairs safely in hand.

Clients

Altogether Hilling Wall has over 70 active clients including potential investors. In terms of size and type, clients range from small start-up businesses to two sizeable companies subject to buy-outs supported by major and well-known bankers. In the case of capital raising requirements, the minimum investment/requirement is £150 000 (only because smaller amounts become uneconomic) although we will consider any proposition if other services are to be included.

IDJ Limited

John D. Incledon/David Comer
IDJ Ltd.
Suite 33
140 Park Lane
London W1Y 3AA

Date of formation: 1972
Organisation type: Private—corporate
* finance*
Geographical area: UK
Matching methods: By judgement of IDJ
* principals*
Investment £ sought: £250 000–£2 million
No. of investors: 400
Successful matches (July 1995–June 1996):
* 2*
Industry preferences: Manufacturing,
* technology and industrial distribution*
Stage of investment: All

Tel.: 0171 499 0355
Fax: 0171 495 1149

Additional services: acquisitions, disposals,
* joint ventures, MBO/MBIs*

Authors' Summary

As one arm of its diverse financial services, IDJ's Angel service attempts to raise finance for unquoted companies, especially manufacturing, technology and service companies that need £2 million–£50 million. This is one of numerous services offered by the company, all on a percentage of investment fee basis.

Company Literature

IDJ has been providing independent corporate finance and advisory services in the UK since its foundation in 1972. Its principals have worked together for more than 10 years and each has over 25 years' experience in his respective profession. Principals lead every assignment.

IDJ agrees detailed written proposals with its clients before any work is undertaken. This discipline has led to the development of innovative solutions and has enabled many clients to achieve their objectives more precisely and cost-effectively than initially anticipated.

IDJ has a broad base of loyal clients both in the UK and overseas. Its primary focus is on transactions in the manufacturing, technology and service fields, where the sums involved are between £2 million and £50 million.

As one of its financial services, IDJ does private placements, where they attempt to raise new finance for unquoted companies, generally equity capital.

In addition to matching entrepreneurs and Business Angels, IDJ performs:

- acquisitions of UK companies and businesses on behalf of UK and overseas purchasers
- disposals on behalf of companies, private individuals and banks
- joint venture/licences in a wide variety of industries and countries
- listings assistance to shareholders on bringing companies to the stock market
- management buy-outs/buy-ins primarily in manufacturing and technology.

Informal Register of Investment Services

Richard Heppenstall
The Informal Register of Investment
  Services
Business Link Calderdale Kirklees
Parkview House
Woodvale Office Park
Woodvale Road
Brighouse
Yorks HD6 4AB

Tel.: 01484 400990
Fax: 01484 710110

Date of formation: 1992
Organisation type: Business Link
Geographical area: West Yorkshire
Matching methods: Matching and bulletin
Investment £ sought: £10 000–£250 000
No. of investors: 79
Successful matches (July 1995–June 1996):
  4
Industry preferences: All
Stage of investment: All
Additional services: Full range of TEC and
  Business Link support services

Authors' Summary

The Informal Register of Investment Services (IRIS) aims to match the preferences of potential investors on their database with investment opportunities submitted by entrepreneurs. IRIS conducts little screening of the investment proposals (which is the responsibility of the potential investors) and is not involved in the negotiation or deal-making processes; its primary aim is to make introductions.

Company Literature

The Informal Register of Investment Services (IRIS) was set up to assist small businesses in West Yorkshire to raise financial capital and gain managerial assistance from private equity investors. IRIS assists both early stage and established firms who wish to raise £10 000 to £250 000.

Upon joining IRIS, potential investors outline their investment preferences. IRIS will then attempt to match these to the specifications of the entrepreneurial ventures that come to them for assistance. To be considered for the service, the venture must have a viable business plan, including financial projections. Many of the potential investors registered with IRIS wish to take a part-time active role in running the firms they invest in.

IRIS only functions as an introduction service, it does not partake in due diligence of the entrepreneurial ventures it features, nor does it attempt to verify information presented by investors or entrepreneurs.

Investors are expected to conduct their own research and seek professional advice in the transaction, negotiation and investment stages. In this way, IRIS offers a specialist service whose primary aim is to introduce potential investors to entrepreneurs.

Inventions

Colin Cramphorn
Inventions
28 Main Street
Mursley
Milton Keynes MK17 0RT

Tel.: 01296 728136
Fax: 01296 720070

E-mail: 100547.1622@compuserve.com

Date of formation: 1991
Organisation type: Licensing inventions
Geographical area: UK, worldwide
Investment £ sought: Inventions to exploit
Industry preferences: None
Stage of investment: Inventions
Additional services: Patent and licensing

Authors' Summary

Inventions offers advice on how to license inventions and other intellectual property concerns. For Invention's advice and assistance, it charges up to 33 per cent of the royalties and revenues arising from the commercial success of the invention.

Company Literature

Inventions is a division of Omega Holdings Limited, a family-owned private company that was incorporated in 1983. Its principal business is licensing, but to function in this very specialised area of business it is necessary to have the skills and resources to deal with several closely associated areas. These may be grouped under the broad headings of presentation, protection, and funding.

Presentation

The standard of presentation of an invention or product to a potential licensee is of course critical to success, but unfortunately it is also an area neglected by most inventors. They after all have an intimate knowledge of their idea and its potential and often assume that the benefits are obvious to others. This is not the case in most instances as the initial assessment of new projects is usually made at a high level where time management is ruthless. If the benefits are not conveyed in a very short space of time the project may not proceed further so we have developed a strong team of designers, illustrators, copy-writers and technical advisers as well as experts able to build models and prototypes so that we can produce the concise material needed to progress the project through to a successful conclusion.

Protection

Protection is an age-old problem to which there is no totally safe conclusion, but we can help to structure a package that will give a reasonable chance of success, bearing in mind available funding. This is a critical area to us also, to the point where we will not become involved unless the intellectual property can be adequately protected. It is, however, important that the various options are carefully considered as timing can be absolutely critical, so under normal circumstances we would prefer to be involved before any patents are filed. We will of course provide suitable agreements for confidential disclosure.

Funding

The seed capital needed to start a project is almost impossible to raise on behalf of an inventor so this usually has to be available from the inventor's own resources or a very close associate. Once the project progresses, a little outside funding becomes possible and we have a network of private and institutional investors hungry for sound propositions.

Moving Forward

Our main expertise is in marketing the opportunity through a team of sales executives and a network of associated agents on an international basis. We have a proven track record of success in a wide range of industries from simple household gadgets to advanced robotics and sophisticated communications technology. We have traditionally attracted innovators through national advertising but this is increasingly being replaced by referrals and recommendations.

The basis on which we work does not usually involve fees, but instead we rely on a share of the income derived from a successful licence agreement. As a result, we have to be very selective and would normally prefer to see at least outline details of the idea before proceeding. If the opportunity looks encouraging we will devote a two-hour period to discuss the proposition and agree an initial plan of action. Up to this stage there will not be any binding commitment by either party other than confidentiality, nor will there be any charges even if the project does not proceed.

ISIS Innovation Ltd

Mrs Maureen Marsh
Administrator
Isis Innovation Limited
2 South Parks Road
Oxford OX1 3UB

Tel.: 01865 272411
Fax: 01865 272412

Date of formation: 1988
Organisation type: Licensing inventions
Geographical area: UK
Investment £ sought: Inventions and
   licensees
Industry preferences: Technology
Stage of investment: Inventions

Authors' Summary

Originally set up to exploit know-how arising out of research conducted at Oxford University and at government-funded Research Councils, Isis Innovation's services are now also available to private individuals who have inventions/research know-how which have commercial potential. Isis Innovation actively seeks licensees who are willing to pay for the rights to intellectual properties and has formed a member society of large industrial firms who are informed regularly, through bulletins and meetings, about new technological findings available for commercialisation.

Company Literature

The University of Oxford established Isis Innovation Limited in 1988 with the help of two initial sponsors from the venture capital sector, Advent and Cogent. The objective of the company is to exploit the results arising from research funded by the UK government through the Research Councils, and by industrial companies, charities and other bodies where the ownership of intellectual property rights remains with the University. It does this by seeking inventions, discoveries and know-how as they arise from the research, then protecting them as appropriate by patent, before trawling for industrial interest in commercialising them. Rewards from exploitation are shared between the inventors, the University and Isis. In 1995/96 research grants and contracts were awarded to the University of Oxford to the value of £104 million, of which some £42 million came from the Research Councils.

Isis seeks licensees to pay lump sums and/or royalties for the use of items of patented technology and know-how arising out of the research. Where it is considered that a spin-off company would produce a better financial return, Isis organises its launch using venture capital or development funding.

Isis was set up primarily to exploit the results of research sponsored by the Research Councils. Its services are also available to members of the University who wish to exploit the results of research funded from other sources, where there are no prior conditions that determine that intellectual property should be exploited by other means, such as by the sponsor. Isis has funds at its disposal for paying the costs of protecting intellectual property rights, and for taking work to the stage at which its full potential can be assessed. Isis believes it to be of benefit to work closely with industrial partners to ensure that new ideas are developed to meet market requirements.

One of Isis's main achievements has been the establishment of The Oxford Innovation Society, which provides efficient access for companies to technology developed at the University. Opportunities are provided to meet with academics across a wide range of disciplines. Communications between Isis and the membership of the Society, which now numbers 50, is both direct and by newsletter. In addition here there are three formal meetings of the Society each year at which leading academics from the University give overview lectures on their own field of science or medicine.

Isis has close links with the Oxford Science Park, which hosts a series of more detailed Seminars for Isis.

Isis has been responsible for launching a number of spin-off companies, including Oxford Molecular Ltd, now listed on the London Stock Exchange, and Oxford Biomedica Ltd, recently floated on the Alternative Investment Market.

LentA Ventures

Robert Cave/Maxine Gooden
LentA Ventures
4 Snow Hill
London EC1A 2BS

Tel.: 0171 236 3000
Fax: 0171 329 0226

E-mail: lenta@itl.net

Date of formation: 1987
Organisation type: Enterprise Agency
Geographical area: London and
* surrounding areas*
Matching methods: Bulletin, database,
* presentations, investor club*
Investment £ sought: £10 000–£250 000
No. of investors: 185
Successful matches (July 1995–June 1996):
* 7*
Industry preferences: All
Stage of investment: All
Additional services: Franchise, start-up,
* and business plan advice*

Authors' Summary

As a division of the London Enterprise Agency, LentA Ventures specialises in assisting entrepreneurs in the London and surrounding areas in raising funding for small early stage firms. LentA Ventures uses the traditional business introduction service techniques to facilitate entrepreneur–investor matching: investment bulletins, computer matching and investment presentations.

Company Literature

LentA Ventures is the informal venture capital arm of the London Enterprise Agency. It is a member of LINC (Local Investment Networking Company) and serves investees and investors in the Greater London area.

LentA Ventures, formerly London LINC, was established in 1987 as a not-for-profit company, with the purpose of assisting businesses to find equity capital through private investors. LentA Ventures has direct access to over 300 private investors through LINC, with a total of over £80 million available for investment. Investors can offer finance and in most cases additional financial, marketing or general management experience, to both start-ups and growth businesses seeking to raise sums between £10 000 and £250 000.

Introductions to investors are made by a combination of the monthly bulletin, live company presentation days and the database matching service.

The monthly bulletin is widely circulated to all registered investors and other financial institutions and intermediaries. This is supported by the database matching service, whereby companies that match specific investor criteria are selected and brought to the attention of particular investors. The company presentation days give selected companies the opportunity to present and discuss their businesses with a large group of private investors.

LentA Ventures is a member of the National LINC and is separately sponsored by the London Enterprise Agency and accountants Kingston Smith.

Local Investment Networking Company (LINC)

Susan Krantz/Irene Robson
LINC
c/o London Enterprise Agency
4 Snow Hill
London EC1A 2BS

Tel.: 0171 236 3000
Fax: 0171 329 0226

E-mail: inform@linc.co.uk
Web site: www.linc.co.uk

Date of formation: 1987
Organisation type: Introduction service
Geographical area: UK
Matching methods: Bulletin and matching
Investment £ sought: £10 000–£250 000
No. of investors: 350
Successful matches (July 1995–June 1996):
51
Industry preferences: All
Stage of investment: Start up, growth,
refinancing
Additional services: Computer database,
investment presentations.

Authors' Summary

Although operating on a national scale, LINC has about a dozen member agencies through which it can deliver services on a local basis. LINC distributes a monthly investment bulletin to potential Business Angel investors (for an annual subscription fee) and also hosts investment presentations where entrepreneurs and Business Angels can meet. Some matching of investment opportunities with potential investors (who are listed on a database) is also provided.

Company Literature

LINC (Local Investment Networking Company) was established in 1987 as a national not-for-profit business introduction service to meet the "equity gap", which is generally considered to be between £10 000 and £250 000.

There are currently over 350 registered LINC investors, and LINC also has access to other national investor networks.

LINC is a "marriage broker" between private investors (Business Angels) and small to medium-sized businesses. LINC has helped raise over £10 million of equity funding for UK businesses. LINC is sponsored by Midland, NatWest, Barclays, The Royal Bank of Scotland, and accountants Kingston Smith.

There are currently 12 LINC member agencies across the country, based at TECs, Business Links and Enterprise Agencies, who all have access to our database of LINC registered investors, representing £80 million. In addition LINC has reciprocal arrangements with other national networks, including the Daily Telegraph Business Network.

LINC offers the following:

• A national network of private investors with £90 million to invest.
• Investors offer not only funding but often managerial expertise, too.
• Comprehensive advice from business advisers at local LINC agencies.
• Especially proactive in promoting businesses to investors by means of bulletins, database, and presentations.
• Access to other national networks of investors.

Those entrepreneurial ventures that are featured in the half page business descriptions in the LINC bulletins are "vetted" by business advisers, based on the comprehensiveness of the business plan, the financial forecasts and, in most cases, meetings with management. For those businesses receiving finance from an LINC registered investor, a fee as a percentage of funds raised may be charged by LINC.

LINC has helped raise over £10 million of equity funding for UK businesses and together with the valuable management skills provided by LINC investors, it is estimated that up to four times as much in extra funding has been sourced from banks and other organisations.

LINC Scotland

David Grahame/Allison Owens
LINC Scotland
30 George Street
Glasgow G2 1EQ

Tel.: 0141 221 3321
Fax: 0141 221 3244

Date of formation: 1993
Organisation type: Enterprise Agency
Geographical area: Scotland
Matching methods: Bulletin, direct
*   networking, computer database*
Investment £ sought: £10 000–£250 000
No. of investors: 350
Successful matches (July 1995–June 1996):
*   20*
Industry preferences: All
Stage of investment: Start-up, growth,
*   refinancing*
Additional services: Business plan advice
*   and for other sources of funds*

Authors' Summary

LINC Scotland is an introduction service that utilises monthly bulletins, investment clubs and forums to match investment opportunities, primarily in Scotland, with investors. LINC Scotland also offers a range of services of value to entrepreneurial firms seeking finance and potential investors.

Company Literature

LINC Scotland is an independent nonprofit-making business introduction service for Business Angels and small firms requiring equity finance. It maintains a close partnership with the Local Investment Networking Company in England and Wales but is constituted differently, being an Enterprise Trust in its own right and closely integrated with other elements of the overall economic development structure in Scotland.

In addition to facilitating individual deals, at least half the Trust's resources go on educational awareness raising and attitude changing activities with small firms as part of the overall aim to greatly increase the recognition and use of informal investment as a tool for growth. This emphasis on stimulating demand arises from the view that, while supply-side encouragement such as tax incentives is welcome, the real inhibition on the growth of this market lies with small firms, too many of whom are still unwilling to use informal investment other than as a last resort.

The operational approach has been to recruit investors to a single national database in order to achieve the necessary critical mass but to adopt a highly flexible approach to local delivery. This may be carried out by the Trust's own employees, secondees from banks or accountancy firms, or staff or consultants directly funded by individual LECs in addition to their central sponsorship of LINC Scotland.

In addition to receiving a regular monthly bulletin and irregular special circulars, every investor member of LINC Scotland is on the invitation list for one of the five regional investor clubs, which meet monthly to be briefed on the latest opportunities in their locality. These clubs are in addition to larger forum type events at which the companies themselves get the chance to present their case for investment, and have proved popular with investors as an opportunity for networking and to address issues of common interest, such as syndication, due diligence and deal structuring. It was discovered early on that computer matching of investors and opportunities is of limited usefulness as informal investment is very much a people business and LINC Scotland concentrates on the personal networking and facilitation skills of its staff. This may also explain the surprising level of success of the investment forums at which, over a two-year period, two out of three companies presenting have secured investment from individuals in the audience.

The LINC Scotland membership covers a wide range of individuals including professional investors acting in effect like private venture capitalists, the classic "serial investors" type usually taking a non-executive position, and a growing number of senior managers leaving industry and looking for employment buy-in opportunities in small manufacturing enterprises.

Mercantile 100

Chris Horne/Douglas McGhee
Kidsons Impey CA
Breckenridge House
274 Sauchiehall Street
Glasgow G2 3EH

Tel.: 0141 307 5000
Fax: 0141 307 5005

Date of formation: 1992
Organisation type: Private—accounting
Geographical area: UK (mostly Scotland)
Matching methods: Matching and
    investment bulletin
Investment £ sought: £10 000–£300 000
No. of investors: 160
Successful matches (July 1995–June 1996):
    3
Industry preferences: All
Stage of investment: All
Additional services: Corporate finance
    advisers and chartered accountants

Authors' Summary

Formerly known as Walkers Chartered Accountants, Kidsons Impey's "Mercantile 100" has a database of potential Business Angel investors who have expressed an interest in investing in small entrepreneurial firms based primarily in Scotland. Based on their investment preferences, Kidsons Impey attempts to match investment opportunities to these potential investors. If a rough match arises, then Kidsons Impey will work with the entrepreneur to formulate a comprehensive business plan for distribution to those investors who fit the match. Their main objective is to make introductions, not to advise on the suitability of investments or on the negotiation and deal-formulation process.

Company Literature

Kidsons Impey has formulated a database, Mercantile 100, of potential private equity investors who are looking for entrepreneurial ventures to fund. The database includes the amount of investment each investor is willing to provide, their preferred geographical area and industry type.

The main objective of Mercantile 100 is to identify business opportunities, primarily based in Scotland, that require equity capital. A personalised service is rendered by Kidsons Impey for each prospective investment proposal. Each investment opportunity is reviewed and assessed on a case by case basis and the strategy for investment is carefully considered. Most investment opportunities featured will seek funding in the £10 000–£300 000 range.

Once a potential investor has been identified, Kidsons Impey will recommend that a Business Funding Appraisal is prepared. This will be in the form of an executive of the proposal, supported by a size and in-depth investigation of the management, financial projections, results and terms of investment. This proposal is then circulated among those investors whose criteria match the firm's features. Further matching and consultation is available on request.

Kidsons Impey provide a personalised matching service, where the main goal is to formulate an entrepreneur–investor introduction. Although consultancy service and advice is offered, specific investment advice is not available. Kidson Impey hopes that its services will facilitate the matching of wealthy private individuals and entrepreneurs in Scotland.

NatWest Angels Service

Keith Bush
NatWest Angels Service
Level 10
Drapers Garden
12 Throgmorton Ave
London EC2N 2DL

Tel.: 0171 454 2236
Fax: 0171 454 2610

Date of formation: 1994
Organisation type: Private—financial
*   service*
Geographical area: UK
Matching methods: personal matching
*   based on predetermined criteria*
Investment £ sought: No min./max. (prefer
*   £20 000+)*
No. of investors: n/a
Successful matches (July 1995–June 1996):
*   n/a*
Industry preferences: All
Stage of investment: All
Additional services: Full range of financial
*   services*

Authors' Summary

NatWest Angels Service is a personalised matching service where the predetermined investment criteria of their Business Angel members are matched with the characteristics of the entrepreneurial ventures seeking finance. The service does not offer investment advice, nor does it get involved post-introduction. Without a particular regional focus, the service aims to match investors and businesses across the UK.

Company Literature

NatWest Angels Service seeks to match potential investors with companies seeking £20 000+ in financial backing. This is conducted through a personalised matching approach which equates the predetermined criteria of the investor on file, with the characteristics of the investment opportunity. Investors will be notified of opportunities matching their previously defined investment criteria.

To be included, an entrepreneurial company must have growth prospects and be willing to release equity and to allow participation by investors. Investors must complete an application form, have a desire to invest and commitment to small manufacturing enterprises investment. The majority of NatWest Angels Service's investors seek to be active in the company in which they invest.

NatWest Angels is in this sense an introduction service only. It has no involvement in subsequent discussions and stresses that all parties must conduct their own due diligence, while no investment recommendations will be made by the service.

If the company seeking funding has an existing banking relationship with NatWest, contact should be made with the branch/business centre where the account is maintained. If the business does not maintain an account with NatWest, contact should be made with an approved intermediary, a list of which can be obtained by calling NatWest Angels Service.

Oxfordshire Investment Opportunity Network

Kate Phelps
Oxfordshire Investment
  Opportunity Network
Oxford Centre for Innovation
Mill Street
Oxford OX2 0JX

Tel.: 01865 790910
Fax: 01865 793165

E-mail: oion@oxtrust.org.uk
Web site: www.oxtrust.org.uk/oion

Date of formation: 1994
Organisation type: Company limited by
  guarantee
Geographical area: Oxfordshire
Matching methods: Presentations, bulletins,
  matching
Investment £ sought: £10 000–£500 000
No. of investors: 130
Successful matches (July 1995–June 1996):
  7
Industry preferences: All
Stage of investment: All, especially early
  stage
Additional services: Business plan
  advice and due diligence pack

Authors' Summary

Through its monthly investment presentations, investment bulletins, database match-ing, and listing of investment opportunities on their Internet site, the Oxfordshire Investment Opportunity Network (OION) aims to stimulate unquoted investments in the Oxfordshire area. As well as offering business advice, especially on entrepreneurial business plans, OION also offers a due diligence pack to ease the research process for potential Business Angel investors.

Company Literature

The Oxfordshire Investment Opportunity Network held its first meeting in April 1994, having been set up with the aim of linking investors with high-growth potential busi-nesses, thereby providing a mechanism for companies to obtain the funding and man-agement expertise they need to grow successfully. To fulfil this aim the Network connects a steady flow of quality companies seeking investment with an established group of active investors who are brought together via presentation meetings and through other less formal contacts.

The target companies for the Network are primarily start-up and early stage com-panies, from all sectors of industry, with a high growth potential. Although businesses from other areas are not discouraged, the focus is on companies based in Oxfordshire, which are expected to grow locally, building jobs and wealth in the county.

Prior to making a presentation, a company or individual seeking investments will be seen by a business adviser from the Heart of England TEC. This provides an oppor-tunity for presenters to receive valuable advice on their business plans and to discuss the contents of their presentation. The business advisers are highly experienced in the field of start-up enterprises and have a thorough understanding of the requirements an investor will have of a project. This plays a vital role in maintaining the quality of the business ideas which came through the Network and, if the adviser feels that a proposal is unsuitable, companies may be filtered out at this stage. In such an instance, every effort is made to offer alternative routes, and constructive criticism of the plans will be offered.

Matching

The main mechanism for matching is provided through Investment Opportunity Presentation Meetings, at which 4–6 companies make 15-minute presentations to an invited audience of investors. The average attendance at these meetings is 40 to 50 people. Information about the opportunities is then circulated to our registered investors and goes on to our Internet site. We have over 130 registered investors.

Alternatively, there is a database match. Investors are targeted with information about companies that may be of interest to them. This is usually done where time is short or confidentiality is a concern.

Legal Document and Due Diligence Pack

The Legal and Due Diligence Pack has been created for Oxfordshire Investment Opportunity Network by Manches & Co and KPMG. The aim is to provide investors and fund-seekers with a guide to the due diligence and legal process associated with private investment in smaller companies. By reducing the costs of the investment process, the pack may be the key to releasing millions of pounds of Business Angel capital to fledgling companies. The pack was launched in November 1996 and is marketed through the Network and Business Links. The proceeds of the pack contribute to the funding of the operating costs of OION.

Principality Financial Management

Peter Phillips/David J. Ward/Fred
Campbell
Principality Financial Management
1st Floor
Alexandra House
1 Alexandra Road
Swansea SA1 5ED

Tel.: 01792 474111
Fax: 01792 474112

Date of formation: 1990
Organisation type: Private—equity broker
Geographical area: UK
Matching methods: Personal matching
Investment £ sought: £50 000–£500 000
No. of investors: 304
Successful matches (July 1995–June 1996):
    3
Industry preferences: All
Stage of investment: All
Additional services: Mergers and
    acquisitions

Authors' Summary

Principality Financial Management (PFM) utilises a personal approach to matching entrepreneurs with Business Angel investors. Upon receipt of a credible business plan, PFM will try to match the opportunity with the preferences of one of the investors listed on their database. Unlike many other Business Angel introduction services, PFM often takes an active role to ensure that the negotiations and the deal are completed successfully. PFM's fee is based on a percentage of the financing they have helped raise.

Company Literature

Principality Financial Management aims to harness the potential arising from a network of Business Angels in situations characterised by a bank's reluctance to get involved and a capital requirement below the traditional venture capital threshold: the classic "equity gap".

PFM works with a base of bona fide Business Angels and is concerned with propositions from the first stages of non-disclosure communication through face-to-face meetings and information gathering to the structuring of a final deal prior to due diligence and completion.

It is worth noting that corporate Business Angels exist in addition to a high network of private individuals. The criteria of each will be different and therefore our matching process is a notional one based on stated requirements and refinements to them over subsequent contact.

PFM finds that it is still the case in a significant number of instances that the plugging of a skills gap within an investee company by a widely experienced Business Angel is as valuable as the actual funding provision. PFM's service spans qualifying start-ups to established businesses. PFM aims to weed out those Business Angels whose substance does not match their claims. PFM works on a "success fee" basis and lends a "personal assessment" approach to the matching of entrepreneurial firms and Business Angels.

Solutions for Scotland

Tinsley Lockhart
Chief Executive
Solutions for Scotland
66/68 Thistle Street
Edinburgh EH2 1EN

Tel.: 0131 225 5000
Fax: 0131 225 2000

E-mail: tinsley@inform.org.uk
Web site: www.inform.org.uk

Date of formation: 1992
Organisation type: MBI introduction and
  strategy consultancy
Geographical area: Scotland/Europe
Matching methods: Personal introduction
Investment £ sought: No min./max.
No. of investors: 300
Successful matches (July 1995–June 1996):
  2
Industry preferences: Internet/multimedia
  and traditional
Stage of investment: All
Additional services: Executive search and
  selection

Authors' Summary

Solutions for Scotland refers its informal investment enquiries to LINC Scotland and offers retained consultancy for those who want to commission research/connections. Solutions for Scotland specialises in Internet/multimedia consultancy and also offers executive search and selection.

Company Literature

Solutions for Scotland is one of Scotland's leading strategists on the development of informal investment, with government and economic development organisations as their main clients. Solutions for Scotland refers all investor/investee enquiries to LINC Scotland in the first instance as Scotland's most effective informal investment network, but also offers retained consultancy on an hourly rate basis for those who want to commission bespoke research/connections. Specialist sector expertise are the Internet/intranet/multimedia design/information management.

Those interested in Solutions for Scotland's services should send a letter in the first instance without a business plan.

Solutions for Scotland also sells an audiotape, *The LINC Scotland Introduction to Informal Investment*, which through interviews of leading professionals and practitioners is a step-by-step guide for both Business Angels and companies looking for investment.

South West Investment Group (SWIG)

John Ager
SWIG
Trevint Ltd
Trevint House
Strangways Villas
Truro
Cornwall TR1 2PA

Tel.: 01872 223883
Fax: 01872 42470

Date of formation: 1992
Organisation type: Private/public—non-profit
Geographical area: Devon and Cornwall
Matching methods: Bulletin, matching, presentations
Investment £ sought: £10 000–£200 000
No. of subscribers: 62
Successful matches (July 1995–June 1996): 10
Industry preferences: All
Stage of investment: All
Additional services: Consultancy, project management and European partnership

Authors' Summary

Managed by the South West Investment Group (SWIG), the Business Link Devon & Cornwall Business Angels Programme (BAP) aims to match potential investors and entrepreneurial businesses in the South West. SWIG distributes an investment opportunity bulletin to its subscribed Business Angels, utilises computer matching software, and holds investment presentations as a means of making entrepreneur Business Angel introductions.

Company Literature

The Business Link Devon & Cornwall Business Angels Programme was set up in 1992 as a pilot programme sponsored and part funded by the DTI. In its endeavour to encourage the development of informal investment networks the government invited TECs to bid for one of five such pilots to be supported for three years. The Devon & Cornwall TEC was successful and appointed the South West Investment Group (then known as Trevint Ltd) to manage the programme on its behalf.

Trevint Ltd was the trading arm of the Cornwall Enterprise Board (CES), a limited by guarantee, not-for-profit investment organisation originally established by Cornwall County Council in 1989. By 1995 the operations of CEB were increasingly involving businesses in Devon so its membership was extended and its name changed to the South West Investment Group. In April 1996 responsibility for the BAP was transferred to the newly established Devon & Cornwall Business Link and this is now reflected in the name of the programme. SWIG remains the contractor for delivering the programme.

The area covered is mostly rural with a long coastline and only two substantial towns, Exeter and Plymouth. It is 160 miles long end to end; the population is 1.5 million; and it has 114 500 small manufacturing enterprises (SMEs), a high proportion of which are farms. Since its inception the BAP has achieved a consistent level of successful matches: 8 in 1992/93, 8 in 1993/94, 12 in 1994/95, 10 in 1995/96 and on course for at least 10 in 1996/97. The average number of proposals submitted to investors is 35 each year.

The total amount of private capital invested to date is £1.8 million. The strengthened balance sheets and improved management have resulted in the banks and other institutions increasing their support, and the funds thereby levered into the recipient companies has been many times larger than the base equity injections.

The pool of investors available to client companies is enhanced by the establishment of links with other networks including LINC, Venture Capital Report, NatWest Angels Service, Daily Telegraph Business Network, VentureNet and Capital Exchange. Efforts are being made to create an integrated network for the whole southwest region, provisionally known as SWAN (South West Angel Network).

As manager of the BAP, SWIG has accumulated a great deal of practical experience. This has been recognised by other publicly supported agencies, resulting in numerous visits by representatives from such organisations seeking to benefit from this experience when setting up similar Business Angel networks. Several visitors from other European countries have also been entertained and SWIG has taken the lead in establishing EBAN (European Business Angels Network) with support from the European Commission.

Talisman Ventures

Angus Forrest/David Smart
Talisman Ventures
24–26 Baltic Street West
London EC1Y 0UL

Tel.: 0171 251 9111
Fax: 0171 251 2609

Date of formation: 1990
Organisation type: Private—interim
  management service
Geographical area: South east/London
  area
Matching methods: Management services
Investment £ sought: £100 000–£1 million+
No. of investors: 380
Successful matches (July 1995–June 1996):
  n/a
Industry preferences: Manufacturing
Stage of investment: Expansion
Additional services: Pre/post investment
  management advice

Authors' Summary

Talisman Ventures offers management services to both passive venture capital investors and to firms seeking finance (usually expansion/growth finance, not start-up capital). Talisman works closely with its client companies to deliver an agreed programme,
be it fund-raising, consultancy or other corporate advice.

Company Literature

Talisman's objective is to help clients build businesses and increase both their profits
and shareholder value at above average rates.

Typical Companies

The client companies usually have sales in the range of £1 million–£10 million p.a. and
are likely to be trading profitably. Where finance is sought, whether by equity, or loan,
or a combination thereof, the sum is likely to be in the range of £100 000 to £1 million
though Talisman will advise management on substantially higher value transactions
such as management buy-outs or acquisitions.

Services

Talisman works closely with its client companies and their existing advisers to deliver
an agreed programme, be it fund-raising, consultancy or other corporate advice.
  Talisman consists of a small and approachable team of specialists. All work is first
agreed with the client and is carried out by experts who have hands-on experience of
working at the highest level, though certain work is undertaken by associates with
particular focused skills. The determination to fulfil a client's requirements and the
willingness to react to new eventualities ensure that procedures remain flexible.

Charges

Charges may be based on time, on a fixed fee or a fixed fee plus a success related
charge. An estimate is given and terms agreed before any project is started and a
breakdown of fees can be provided before and during an assignment.

Clients

Talisman works for both investors who want to invest money and investee companies that want to raise money. However, to avoid a conflict of interest it never works for both parties in a single transaction.

A Fuller Explanation of the Fund-raising Service

Talisman will look carefully at the current position, consider the goals and, having established details of the company's structure, will advise on all aspects of fund-raising and recommend how this would be best achieved—whether by loan or equity capital.

Management of fund-raising is complex, particularly for the inexperienced. Anyone who has been involved in this type of work in the past will appreciate why two heads are better than one. The areas requiring skills are:

- identifying the right potential investors
- presenting the offer and persuading those investors to participate
- negotiating the terms and conditions
- managing the transaction including dealing with other professionals.

Talisman handles the whole process and, furthermore, is experienced in the management of the legal, accountancy and verification work required, which it can carry out independently or in tandem with the client's existing accountants and lawyers.

TEChINVEST

Vivienne Upcott Gill
TEChINVEST
South and East Cheshire TEC Ltd and
 Business Link
PO Box 37
Dalton Way
Middlewich
Cheshire CW10 0HU

Tel.: 01606 737009/734288
Fax: 01606 734201

Date of formation: 1993
Organisation type: TEC/Business Link
Geographical area: Primarily Cheshire
Matching methods: Bulletin, presentations
Investment £ sought: £3000–£500 000
No. of investors: 90 (and 1000+ reciprocal)
Successful matches (July 1995–June 1996):
 8
Industry preferences: All
Stage of investment: All
Additional services: Advice service, legal
 documentation and training workshop

Authors' Summary

TEChINVEST aims to match local Business Angels with entrepreneurial firms seeking finance. It offers these small firms advice on business plan formulation and then distributes a bulletin of these investment opportunities to local investors. TEChINVEST also offers an advice service for entrepreneurs, investment presentations and training workshops.

Company Literature

TEChINVEST is an innovative programme designed originally to facilitate successful investment in growing businesses in Cheshire and the Wirral. TEChINVEST provides an extensive range of services for local companies and entrepreneurs seeking long-term loan and/or equity finance to develop or expand their business and for private individuals, company investors and venture capital fund managers, whatever their location who are seeking investment opportunities in businesses. It aims not only to link companies and investors, but also to provide them with the knowledge, support and contacts to form long-term successful business "marriages" based on sound business proposals. Key features of the TEChINVEST programme are an advisory service for companies seeking investment, an investors club, and practical workshops open to anyone interested in practical advice and information on the mysteries, issues and experiences of involvement in the investment business.

TEChINVEST was founded with support from the Department of Trade and Industry, by Cheshire's three Training and Enterprise Councils (TECs)—South and East Cheshire TEC, CEWTEC and NORMIDTEC—all non-profit-making private companies limited by guarantee, whose objectives are to encourage and facilitate wealth and growth in the local economy. It continues to be funded largely from sponsorship by these and other TECs in the North West.

Since TEChINVEST was launched in February 1993 the service has stimulated investment interest in many of the projects it has promoted and has already seen a number of investment deals concluded as a result of its services.

By Summer 1994, approximately £1.1 million had been invested in 22 deals in 13 TEChINVEST client businesses by venture capital fund members and by, and through, private individual and company investor members of the TEChINVEST Investors Club or associated investor networks. Individual investments as loan and/or equity ranged from £3000 to £30 000 from individual investors, some investing alongside others to make a bigger total investment for individual companies; £500 000 was invested in one company by a venture capital fund member. Additionally offers of investment totalling approximately £1.5 million had been received. Many of the client companies have also raised additional finance from other sources, in some cases triggered by the investor interest through TEChINVEST.

The TEChINVEST Advisory Service is available to established companies and start-up businesses wishing to raise long-term finance. Companies using the service will have a sound business plan that demonstrates good potential for growth and profit and evidence of company or personal track record. They will have a positive interest in releasing equity and will normally be looking for an investment of between £10 000 and £250 000. The advisory service aims to increase the likelihood of such businesses successfully raising long-term finance through equity and/or loan by evaluating the attractiveness of the proposal to potential investors, providing appropriate specialist support to improve the presentation of the case, publicising the opportunity initially to local investors, but as widely as possible to known investors throughout the UK, and presenting the proposal to an investors club meeting if appropriate.

Venture Capital Report

James Mallinson
Venture Capital Report Ltd
The Magdalen Centre
Oxford Science Park
Oxford OX4 4GA

Tel.: 01865 784411
Fax: 01865 784412

E-mail: vcr@vcr1978.demon.co.uk
Web site: www.demon.co.uk/vcr1978

Date of formation: 1978
Organisation type: Private—investment
  opportunities network
Geographical area: UK, some international
Matching methods: Magazine, investor
  presentations
Investment £ sought: £10 000–£1 million
No. of investors: 748
Successful matches (July 1995–June 1996):
  22
Industry preferences: All
Stage of investment: All
Additional services: Workshops, free
  investment presentations, publisher of
  The VCR Guide to Venture Capital in
  the UK & Europe

Authors' Summary

As the oldest and largest business introduction service in the UK, Venture Capital Report (VCR) has raised more than £16 million for about 190 companies over the last 19 years. VCR offers a number of services to link entrepreneurial businesses with potential Business Angel investors. In addition to a monthly investment opportunity magazine (which can feature 15+ detailed investment opportunities per issue), VCR also advises entrepreneurs on how to prepare a good business plan, holds monthly investment presentations, and offers investment workshops for both entrepreneurs and Business Angels.

Company Literature

Venture Capital Report (VCR) was founded in 1978, and is the longest established business introduction service in the UK. There are a number of key differences between it and other services.

The detailed articles (five pages) on each business published in the Report are written by experienced VCR staff after appraising the business plan and meeting the entrepreneurs concerned. Articles are not written by the entrepreneur, but they are sent drafts for approval and any reasonable changes. Alternatively, like most other services, entrepreneurs can write their own one-page advertisement (about 500 words). In this case there is no need to meet, nor is a success fee charged. The entrepreneur's contact address and telephone number is published at the end of each article, enabling investors to make direct contact, as opposed to the normal practice of replying to box numbers for further information. Full financial data (i.e. balance sheet, profit and loss account, projections and use of funds) and a suggested financial structure (i.e. percentage of equity for capital sought) are provided in each article, which also gives full CVs of the management, a description of the product or service, its market, the competition, and any photographs.

VCR's 700+ subscribers are the largest group of Business Angels in the UK. They pay the most expensive subscription (£350 p.a.), which deters timewasters and ensures that subscribers are genuinely interested in investing.

VCR has a database of subscribers' investment preferences, which it uses to try to alert them to suitable proposals in the Report. VCR also promotes its business propositions to a wider audience at no extra cost. For example, VCR distributes monthly summaries (an anonymous 100-word description of each business) to a circulation list of 3000. It advertises a one-line description of each business in the *Financial Times* and *The Economist*, and, where appropriate, it tries to attract national media coverage for businesses that may also attract investors.

The timing of the process is relatively quick. Entrepreneurs need to meet with VCR by the 15th of the month, as it goes to press on the 20th. The article is then published in the Report on the 1st of the following month, with a short (150-word) summary published in the subsequent issue.

VentureNet

Sue Grant/John List
VentureNet
The Enterprise Support Group Ltd
Albury Hall
The Street
Albury
Guildford
Surrey GU5 9AD

Tel.: 01483 205008
Fax: 01483 205009

E-mail: ops@enterprisesupport.co.uk
Web site: www.esg.co.uk

Date of formation: 1994
Organisation type: Private—electronic
  publisher of investment opportunities
Geographical area: UK
Matching methods: Publishes investment
  opportunities on the Internet
Investment £ sought: £20 000–£1 million
No. of investors: 1000+
Successful matches (July 1995–June 1996):
  n/a
Industry preferences: All
Stage of investment: All
Additional services: Postal printout of
  investment opportunities

Authors' Summary

VentureNet provides a computer database of investment opportunities that potential investors (Business Angels) can access on the Internet, by means of their own personal computer. If a potential investor wishes to initiate contact with the entrepreneur, the investor indicates interest and after the entrepreneur has had the opportunity to make a check on the investor, an introduction will be established by the entrepreneur. This allows the entrepreneur to "stay in the driving seat". A postal printout of the opportunities is also available.

Company Literature

The objective of VentureNet is to provide the fragmented, localised Business Angel networks with the independent, national system and quality standards necessary to establish private equity funding as a mature and professional element within the corporate finance portfolio.

VentureNet was designed by an advisory board composed of experienced and active private investors (Business Angels) and business people—who used all available means of locating potential investments and all existing introduction services. It was led by highly experienced Enterprise Support Group staff (ex 3i plc) and had the benefit of input from the country's acknowledged leading academic researcher on the subject.

The format and content of the information on the VentureNet database are those requested by investors—no more, no less—to enable them to make an initial appraisal of available investment opportunities before committing valuable time to further investigation.

VentureNet is still the only national, on-line database of Investment opportunities which comply with a published Information Quality Standard.

Identification of individuals presenting investment opportunities is not possible directly from the database. This has to be obtained from the introducer of the opportunity. That might be a Business Link, a TEC, an accountant, or consultants representing their clients. This process keeps the introducer in the driving seat and enables a check to be made on the investor before any introduction is effected.

The database can be interrogated from software loaded on to an investor's own computer, at any time, using personalised and easily modified search criteria. It can also be examined by an investor, or a representative, via Enterprise Support Group's Internet site using a password from VentureNet.

The cost of placing an investment opportunity on the VentureNet database for six months is £90.00 + VAT.

VentureNet is available on the Internet through the Enterprise Support Group's Web site: http://www.esg.co.uk. As the joint venture between The Enterprise Support Group UK (ESG/UK) and The Enterprise Support Group United States (ESG/US) develops, it will include mergers, acquisitions, joint ventures and strategic alliances—as well as investments.

Winsec Corporate Exchange

Christopher Meynell
Winsec Corporate Exchange
Winsec Financial Services Ltd.
1 The Centre
Church Road
Tiptree
Colchester
Essex CO5 0HF

Tel.: 01621 815047
Fax: 01621 817965

Date of formation: 1992
Organisation type: Private—corporate
Geographical area: East Anglia
Matching methods: Investment bulletin
Investment £ sought: £30 000–£2 million
No. of investors: 150
Successful matches (July 1995–June 1996):
   4
Industry preferences: All
Stage of investment: All
Additional services: Sale/purchase of firms;
   retained purchaser searches; business
   plans and management consultancy;
   investment, pension and tax advice

Authors' Summary

Winsec Corporate Exchange (WCE) distributes a free bulletin of unquoted investment opportunity summaries to potential Business Angel investors. Fees are paid only upon funding success. The Winsec company has three divisions, which deal in Business Angel finance, financial advice, and business consulting.

Company Literature

The WCE is a business funding introductory service operating as the third leg of the Winsec group of companies. The main constituent of the group offers an independent financial advisory service and is registered with the PIA.

WCE was formed to assist small and medium-sized enterprises in their search for external equity finance. Databases of companies seeking funds and of individuals and companies seeking unquoted investment opportunities are maintained, and where appropriate the two are matched.

There are no fees for a search registration with WCE as fees are charged on a success only basis to the company seeking funding. The basis is 5 per cent on the first £500 000, 4 per cent on the next £1 million and thereafter negotiable with a minimum fee of £5000, payable at the point of receipt of investment funds.

Projects submitted to WCE gain the benefits of a focused matching service. Initially after the terms have been agreed, a synopsis of the project business is produced and agreed with the company. This is sent to potential investors as an unidentifiable "taster" with a Letter of Confidentiality. For those who request further information and a business plan, the Letter of Confidentiality is first signed and returned.

WCE employs various routes to seek out potential investors. First, registered investors are selected and targeted on the basis of rough investment criteria. Secondly, WCE publishes a periodic *Investment Opportunities Bulletin*. This contains brief summaries of projects and their requirements. This is circulated to our full database of potential sources of around 1500 accountants, solicitors and corporate finance specialists, who themselves have access to a wide range of investors.

WCE broadens the search for investors still further by using other venture capital networks with whom links have been established. One of these is the NatWest Angel Service—a computer matching facility—for which WCE is one of three private sector intermediaries. Submitting projects to this service is a free extension of the funding search service.

WCE has extended its activities with companies by providing a merger, acquisition and sale service. While the terms are similar to those set out for fund-raising, there may be occasions when fee terms are negotiated with those seeking to invest or purchase businesses. This provides WCE with improved access to potential corporate Business Angels.

Yorkshire Association of Business Angels

Ian McNeill
Yorkshire Association of Business
  Angels
15 The Haywain
Ilkley
West Yorkshire LS29 8SL

Tel.: 01943 817132
Fax: 01943 817892

E-mail: 100623.3023.compuserve.com

Date of formation: 1995
*Organisation type: Private—business
  introduction service*
*Geographical area: Yorkshire and north
  UK*
*Matching methods: Investment bulletin
Investment £ sought: £20 000–£150 000*
No. of investors: 40
*Successful matches (July 1995–June 1996):
  3*
Industry preferences: All
Stage of investment: All

Authors' Summary

The Yorkshire Association of Business Angels is a private business introduction service which caters primarily to the Yorkshire region. It holds an extensive database of potential investors and uses a bulletin and investment presentation meetings to match entrepreneurial investment opportunities with these investors.

Company Literature

The Yorkshire Association of Business Angels (YABA) maintains a database of members that contains only the information a member (potential investor) has agreed to have shared. The purpose of the database is to allow any details of potential investment opportunities to be circulated to members. YABA will then act as a clearing house to establish contact between interested parties. In this respect, the details held in the database will only be supplied to other members, and to no one else without their express permission.

Investment opportunities may range from as little as £10 000 up to several hundred thousand pounds which may be syndicated and include a combination of Angel money, founder shares, venture capital and bank debt. Typically, a business suitable for investment from the Yorkshire Angel community will have one or more of the following characteristics:

- Located within a reasonable travelling distance of the potential investor's home.
- Unable to raise capital from a bank (because of limited security) or conventional venture capital (because the opportunity may be too small, at too early a stage, too high risk, etc.).
- Requires the business experience of an investor as well as their money, not only to provide operational management, but also to provide credibility and expertise.

Opportunities are brought to YABA by virtue of its growing reputation and through the professional community throughout the region.

YABA has two classes of membership:

- "Full" member—those with a genuine desire and capability to invest personal funds in business ventures.

- "Associate members"—typically professional firms who are able to provide a source of potential deals.

Members are discouraged from selling their services to other members, or attending meetings as a way of simply securing consulting business.

With the above exception, there are no rules and regulations that govern the association. YABA actively encourages informality and networking without the restrictions that exist in other commercial frameworks. However, confidentiality is important, and no opportunity is discussed at YABA meetings without the specific consent of the principals and/or their advisers.

YABA meetings are held every two months in convenient venues in the region, normally starting at 6.00 p.m. and lasting for approximately two hours. Many meetings carry on informally until late evening owing to interest generated by the opportunities discussed.

NOTES

1. Some of the typologies stated in this chapter are based on research reported in Harrison and Mason (1995) and the British Venture Capital Association 1995/6 Report on Business Angel Investment Activity.
2. The Financial Services Act 1986 in fact may prohibit many BISs from carrying on these types of activities. See the chapter by Jim Clarke on "Business introduction services in the United Kingdom and the Financial Services Act 1986", in Harrison and Mason (1996).
3. This typology is partially based on the article "Developing the informal venture capital market: is there still a role for public sector business introduction services?" by Harrison and Mason (1995).
4. For further information on Business Angel–entrepreneur intermediaries in the UK, see the following publications:

The Venture Capital Report Guide to Venture Capital in the UK & Europe
Venture Capital Report Ltd
FREEPOST (OF2375)
Oxford OX4 4YZ
Tel.: 01865 784411, Fax: 01865 784412

This is probably the most comprehensive guide available on business introduction services and venture capital firms in the UK and Europe—a useful guide for entrepreneurs, Business Angels, and venture capitalists; over 1300 pages.

BVCA Sources of Business Angel Capital 1996/97
British Venture Capital Association, Essex House, 12–13 Essex Street, London WC2R 3AA
Tel.: 0171 240 3846, Fax: 0171 240 3849

This is a guide to business introduction services in the UK, but it does not include a listing of venture capital firms.

For a more academic analysis of business introduction services, see the following book:

Informal Venture Capital: Evaluating the Impact of Business Introduction Services
Edited by Richard Harrison and Colin Mason, 1996
Woodhead-Faulkner (Publishers) Limited (a division of Simon & Schuster)

For book purchase, contact: Professor Colin Mason, Department of Geography, University of Southampton, Southampton SO17 1BJ
Tel.: 01703 592217/5, Fax: 01703 593729/593295.

VENTURE CAPITAL FIRMS THAT WILL CONSIDER INVESTING LESS THAN £100 000

Venture capital firms act as principals and manage institutional or in-house money, which they invest in unquoted companies. The investment criteria and the process of raising finance may be more rigorous than for a Business Angel. All of the following information is taken directly from BVCA: Sources of Business Angel Capital 1996/97

Venture capital firm	Amount of investment considered			Start-up/early stage and some seed considered	Industry sectors considered	Geographical preferences	Head office telephone number
	Av. £000s	Min. £000s	Max. £00s				
Abel Venture Managers Ltd	250	50	500	No	All. Specialises in electronics, communications and computer related	UK	01374 470373
British Steel (Industry) Ltd	50	20	150	Yes	Mainly manufacturing and related service businesses	Traditional steel areas in UK	0114 273 1612
Business Link Doncaster	75	50	100	Yes	All	South Yorkshire	01302 761000
Cambridge Research & Innovation Ltd	100	20	200	Yes	Technology protected by intellectual property rights	East Anglia, East Midlands	01223 312856
Centreway Development Capital Ltd	100	50	150	Yes	All	UK	01675 466796
Compass Investment Management Ltd	–	Open	500	Yes	All	North America, UK	0171 409 0014
Derbyshire Enterprise Board Limited	200	50	250	No	All except retail and property	Derbyshire, East Midlands	01246 207390
Egan & Talbot Capital Limited	77	20	150	Yes	All	UK, East Anglia, N Home Counties	01480 812218
Enterprise Equity Capital Limited	300	50	750	Yes	All	North Ireland only	01232 242500
Equity Ventures Ltd	100	25	500	Yes	All	England	0117 931 1318
Fife Enterprise	30	5	50	Yes	Computer, electronics, biotech, medical, health, chemical, manufacturing, services	Scotland, Fife only	01592 623000
Industrial Development Board for Northern Ireland	Open	Open	Open	Yes	Manufacturing and tradable services only	Northern Ireland	01232 233233
Lancashire Enterprise Board	150	2	750	Yes	All	North West England	01772 203020

Name					Sector	Region	Telephone
London Ventures (Fund Managers) Ltd	73	5	150	Yes	Communications, computer, consumer, environment, industrial, leisure, media, medical, manufacturing, services	Greater London only	0171 316 1010
Lothian Enterprises Ltd	150	10	250	Yes	All	Scotland, Lothian region	0131 220 2100
Loxko Venture Managers Ltd	210	Open	500	Yes	Chemical, construction, energy, environmental, financial services, industrial, medical, manufacturing, services, transport	UK and Western Europe	0171 240 5024
Midland Enterprise Fund for the South East	80	25	150	Yes	All	Sussex, Surrey, Kent, Hants	01273 835455
Midlands Venture Fund Managers Ltd	75	20	125	Yes	All	East and West Midlands	0115 967 8400
Northern Enterprise (Manager) Ltd	52	5	100	Yes	Biotech, chemical, communications, computer, consumer, energy, environmental, industrial, leisure, electronics, manufacturing, services, transport	Cleveland, Co. Durham, Tyne & Wear, Northumberland	0191 233 1892
Prelude Technology Investments Limited	700	10	1500	Yes	Biotech, chemical, communications, computer, consumer, industrial, medical, electronics, manufacturing	UK	01954 288090
Scottish Enterprise	350	50	1000	Yes	Biotech, computer, energy, industrial, medical, health, electronics, manufacturing, food, software, consumer, services	Scotland	0141 248 2700
Seed Capital Limited	150	5	250	Yes	Innovative engineering/science	England, within one hour of Oxford	01865 784466
South West Investment Group Ltd	75	25	150	Yes	All	Cornwall and Devon	01872 223883
Transatlantic Capital Ltd	—	25	750	Yes	Biotech, environmental, medical	North America, UK, W. Europe	0171 436 1216
Ulster Development Capital Ltd	250	50	400	Yes	All	Northern Ireland	01232 246765
Yorkshire Enterprise Group (Yorkshire Fund Managers Ltd)	87	30	1000	Yes	Chemical, computer, consumer, industrial, leisure, electronics, manufacturing	Yorkshire and Humberside	0113 294 5050

Source: British Venture Capital Association, Essex House, 12–13 Essex Street, London WC2R 3AA. Tel.: 0171 240 3846; fax: 0171 240 3849

Glossary

accounts receivable The money owed to a firm for products/services sold on credit. Accounts receivable are shown as current assets on the firm's balance sheet.

advertising Any paid form of nonpersonal persuasive message delivered through mass media.

AIM Alternative Investment Market. A London Stock Exchange market that allows small growing companies to raise capital and have their shares traded in a market without full market listing.

amortisation Regarding debt financing, this is making a scheduled series of periodic payments over the life of the debt and its interest. It provides for the gradual retirement of the principal.

articles of partnership A legal agreement between partners that specifies the responsibilities, role, involvement, and duties of each of the partners.

asset Something of value owned by the firm.

asset-backed loan A loan made with assets of the firm as collateral. Assets typically involved may include machinery, equipment or occasionally accounts receivable or inventory.

BES Business Expansion Scheme. A scheme intended to encourage high tax payers to invest in small business, by allowing them to offset the investment (up to £40,000 per annum) against their top rate of tax. In practice, the scheme became a tax avoidance measure and it was ended in 1993. In 1994 BES was replaced by *EIS*.

bonded warehouse An independent, insured, public warehouse that will not release stored items without presentation of an issued warehouse receipt. These are popular with lenders who must maintain close control over finished goods inventory that a borrower has pledged as collateral for a loan.

break-even point The level of activity where sales revenue is just equal to operating expenses; that is, the sales volume is such that a net operating income of zero results.

budget A plan expressed in numerical terms—for example, units of product in production budget, revenues and expenses in a sales budget, or cash inflows and outflows in a cash budget.

Business Angel Informal suppliers of *risk capital*.

business concept As used in a business plan, the business concept is a statement summarising the product or service, how it will meet the needs of its target market, what will be its sustainable competitive advantage, and what resources are needed to achieve its goals.

business description The part of the business plan that provides the reader with a summary of the plan's key points and conclusions.

business introduction service Organisations that help Business Angels find suitable companies to invest in, and vice versa. Usually, business introduction services do no more than introduce the parties.

Business Link Government-funded referral service that also offers advice to small and medium-sized businesses.

business plan A detailed plan stating the objectives of a business over a certain period, typically one, three or five years.

business risk The uncertainty surrounding the firm's ability to generate sales, cash flows and earnings.

buy-in The purchase of a holding of more than 50 per cent in a company by people from outside the firm, who wish to run it.

buy-out The purchase of a company by managers, usually with the help of venture capitalists.

capital structure The mix of long and short-term debt and owner's equity capital used to finance the firm's fixed assets.

cash budget A financial planning tool showing the period to period estimates of the amount and timing of expected cash flows.

cash discount A reduction from the stated price on the invoice of a good or service for early payment.

channels of distribution The means by which a producer gets their product to the end customer. For example, a middleman and a retailer. New channels of distribution can substantially change the dynamics of an industry.

collateral Assets that have been pledged to secure a loan. The lender holds a lien on the assets and can claim them in the event the borrower defaults.

contribution format income statement An alternative format income statement that classifies costs, variable and fixed, by their relationship to sales.

Corporate Angels Companies which make Angel-type investments. They have corporate resources at their disposal and tend to invest greater levels of funds than most individual Angel investors. They invest predominantly for financial gain.

corporation A legal and taxable entity that has life, existence, duties, and responsibilities separate and distinct from its stockholders.

current assets The assets of the firm consisting of cash, or the assets expected to turn over or be converted into cash in less than one year.

deal flow Number of investment deals considered by a Business Angel per year. Depends on an Angel referral network and quality of introduction service used.

debt capital Funds borrowed under a legally binding contract that requires, among other possible enforceable provisions, the payment of interest and repayment of principal.

declining industries Industries on their way out; competition may be intense for diminishing revenues with profit margins under great pressure. Typically, customers are turning to other solutions to meet their needs.

dividends Distribution of profits to shareholders.

due diligence Detailed research into the entrepreneur, key personnel and the background to the business to assess its future and risk for investment.

EIS Enterprise Investment Scheme—a government initiative that offers income tax relief on equity investments in unquoted companies. This helps small businesses raise capital without having to become listed on the Stock Exchange. EIS was started in 1994 to replace *BES*.

emerging industries Industries where many new ventures are the norm. These are new industries where the industry structure is yet to be established. Often a significant amount of time is spent by industry pioneers doing missionary work—helping customers new to the industry to understand the way products/services meet previously unmet and/or understood needs.

Entrepreneur Angels The most active and experienced informal investors. They represent a particularly appealing source of finance for the first-time entrepreneur.

equity capital Ownership funds which represent a proportionate claim on the firm's cash flows and profits.

equity gap Where a small company needs finance beyond what the entrepreneur can raise by him or herself, but funds can't be sought from banks or venture capitalists because the company is unproven. This gap can be filled by Business Angels.

factoring The sale of the firm's account receivables to specialised financial institutions known as factors, in order to raise funds.

financial lease A lease contract used in a leasing of business assets. It has the characteristics of a debt plan.

financial plan The plan that reflects the amount of financing needed to make operating plans feasible, when and in what form the financing is needed, and who will be approached for the needed funds.

financial risk The uncertainty surrounding the firm's ability to generate the cash flows needed to meet its contractual financial obligations.

financial success A firm that generates a level of cash flow and profit sufficient to compensate its owner(s) for the investment, time, effort and risk assumed is a financial success.

fixed assets The firm's long-term assets such as land, buildings, and equipment.

flotation "Going public"—inviting the public to buy shares in the company. After flotation the shares can be traded on a stock exchange. This is one way that owners of a company can raise new capital or liquidate their investments. Flotation can be through the main market or the Alternative Investment Market (*AIM*).

free cash flow Cash flow remaining after meeting operating needs, debt service, the replacement of assets, and dividend payments.

general partnership An association of two or more persons to conduct business as co-owners. Each general partner has management equality and unlimited personal liability for the debts of the partnership.

going public See *flotation*.

growth capital The long-term financing needed to finance additions to the firm's fixed asset base.

growth industries Industries that are enjoying rapid growth as customers begin to recognise the need for the product/service. These are new industries where the industry structure is beginning to be established—often a very good place for new ventures.

Income Seeking Angels Active individual investors who have made one or two low level investments over the past three years. They are well-off, but not as wealthy as the other Angel types. They make their investments both for financial gain and to generate a job/income for themselves.

industry The group of businesses supplying related products or services and the complementary businesses that support them.

industry analysis A key component of the business plan, which focuses on the current state of the industry and its future directions.

industry life cycle The theory that industries go through a life cycle, similar to a product life cycle, with four major phases: introduction, growth, maturity and decline.

inventory The current assets that will be converted into saleable products, those that have been partially converted into saleable products, or those finished products available for resale. Inventory is shown on the firm's balance sheets as raw materials, work-in-progress, or finished goods.

just-in-time inventory system An inventory system designed to reduce inventory costs by having suppliers ship parts and raw materials as they are needed.

Latent Angels Inactive Angels who have made one or more informal investments in the past, but who have remained inactive for at least the past three years. They are very wealthy, self-made, private individuals, with substantial funds available to invest, and who are now interested in making informal investments. Of all the Angel types, Latent Angels are the most concerned with venture location.

LBO Leveraged buy-out.

leveraged buy-out The purchase of one company by another or by individuals through the use of borrowed funds.

lien A lender's legal claim for the borrower's assets that have been pledged as collateral for a loan.

mature industries Industries that have arrived—the industry structure is relatively well established with competitors understanding each others' strengths, weaknesses and market position.

missionary selling The marketing and sales activities that take place when a product class is new to the market. At this stage a firm is just trying to convince people to use a product/service.

pro forma statements Financial statements that contain estimated figures for a forthcoming financial period.

quoted company A company listed with the London Stock Exchange.

return on investment An annual calculation of the return from an Angel's investment. Realised return occurs after the investment is cashed in. Potential return is an estimate forecasting the future cash-in value.

risk capital Capital invested in a company when there is a high degree of risk, such as in a company that is just starting or expanding.

ROI Return on investment.

segmentation The way a firm chooses to divide up its market in order to be able to focus its marketing efforts. Examples of potential segmentation bases include: usage, demographics, geography, and psychographics.

target market A simple, yet powerful idea: out of all the potential segments the target market is the one which your firm targets as your primary focus.

TEC Training and Enterprise Council—an organisation of local employers and civil servants that oversee training schemes relevant for the locality. TECs also promote informal investment through the *Business Link* Network.

unquoted company A company that is not listed with the London Stock Exchange.

unique selling proposition (USP) The compelling reasons you are offering your potential customers in order to encourage them to buy from you.

venture capitalist An individual, company or organisation that invests in another company.

Virgin Angels That group of inactive investors who have not yet made an investment in an unquoted venture. They are private individuals who are looking to provide finance to new or growing businesses, with a view to creating a job or a regular income for themselves, and to earn higher returns than those available on the stock market. Virgin Angels are not as wealthy as active Business Angels and have less funds available to invest. They do not cite this lack of funds as restricting their investment activity, but instead point to an absence of suitable investment proposals.

Wealth Maximising Angels This group of active Angel investors comprise wealthy private individuals who have made several investments in new and growing ventures. They tend to be very wealthy though without being quite as rich as Entrepreneur Angels and they make their investments primarily for financial gain.

References

Aaker, D. (1994) *Managing Brand Equity*. London: Free Press.

Aaker, D. (1996) *Building Strong Brands*. London: Free Press.

Abrams, Rhonda (1993) *The Successful Business Plan: Secrets and Strategies*. Grants Pass, Oregon: Oasis Press.

Arum, J. (1989) "Attitudes and behaviours of informal investors toward early-stage investments, technology-based ventures and coinvestors", *Journal of Business Venturing*, vol. 4, pp. 333–47.

Atkin, R. and Esiri, M. (1993) "Informal investment–investor and investee relationships", paper delivered to the 16th National Small Firms' Policy and Research Council, 16 November.

Avendi, R. (1994) *Hypercompetition*. London: Free Press.

Baty, G. (1991) *Entrepreneurship for the 1990s*. Englewood Cliffs, NJ: Prentice-Hall.

BVCA (1992, 1993, 1994) *A Directory of Business Introduction Services*. London: British Venture Capital Association.

Cary, L. (1995) *Venture Capital Report Guide to Venture Capital in the UK and Europe*, 7th edn. Henley-on-Thames: Venture Capital Report Ltd.

Cary, L. (1996) "Venture capital report: achievements and lessons from an investment bulletin service", in R. Harrison and C. Mason (eds), *Informal Venture Capital: Evaluating the Impact of Business Introduction Services*. London: Prentice Hall.

CBI (1993) "Finance for growth: meeting the financing needs of small and medium enterprises", *A Report of the Confederation of British Industry (CBI) Smaller Firms Council*. London: CBI.

Chernatony, L. de and McDonald, M. (1992) *Creating Powerful Brands*. Oxford: Butterworth Heinemann.

Churchill, Neil C. (1997) "Mastering Enterprise 8: the six phases of company growth", *Financial Times*, 20 January.

Churchill, Neil C. and Lewis, Virginia L. (1983) "The five stages of small business growth", *Harvard Business Review*, May–June.

Cooper, R. (1993) *Winning at New Products: Accelerating the Process from Idea to Launch*, 2nd edn. Wokingham: Addison Wesley.

DeThomas, A. and Fredenberger, W. (1995) *Writing a Convincing Business Plan*. Hauppauge, New York: Barron's Business Library.

Dixon, R. (1991) "Venture capitalists and the appraisal of investments", *Omega*, vol. 9, pp. 333–44.

Ennew, C. and Binks, M. (1993) "Financing entrepreneurship in recession: does the banking relationship constrain performance?", paper presented to the 13th Babson Entrepreneurship Research Conference, University of Houston.

Fiet, J. (1995) "Reliance upon informants in the venture capital industry", *Journal of Business Venturing*, vol. 10, pp. 195–223.

Freear, J., Sohl, J. and Wetzel, W. (1994) "Angels and non-angels: are there differences?", *Journal of Business Venturing*, vol. 9, pp. 109–23.

Gaston, R. (1989) *Finding Private Venture Capital for your Firm: A Complete Guide.* New York: Wiley.

Gilmore, J. and Pine, J. (1997) "The four faces of mass customization: the new frontier in business competition", *Harvard Business Review*, January–February.

Goodman, J. and Allen, K. (1992) "The credit crunch: are federal policies putting entrepreneurial firms on a debt diet?", paper presented at the 12th Babson Entrepreneurial Research Conference, INSEAD, Fontainbleau.

Hamel, G. and Prahalad, C.K. (1996) *Competing for the Future.* Boston, MA: Harvard Business School Press.

Harrigan, K. (1980) *Strategies for Declining Businesses.* Lexington, MA: Lexington Books.

Harrison, R. and Mason, C. (1992) "The roles of investors in entrepreneurial companies: a comparison of informal investors and venture capitalists", *Venture Finance Research Project Working Paper No. 5*, University of Southampton and University of Ulster.

Harrison, R. and Mason, C. (1995) "Developing the informal venture capital market: is there still a role for public sector business introduction services?", paper presented to the ESRC Seminar on New Developments in the Finance of New and Small Firms, University of Paisley, Craigie Campus, Ayr, 28–29 March.

Harrison, R. and Mason, C. (1996) *Informal Venture Capital: Evaluating the Impact of Business Introduction Services.* London: Prentice Hall.

Hay, M. and Abott, S. (1993) "Investing for the future: promoting seed, start-up and early stage venture capital funding of new technology-based firms in the UK", a report commissioned by Advent Limited, London.

Kotha, S. (1995) "Mass customization: implementing the emerging paradigm for competitive advantage", *Strategic Management Journal*, Summer.

Kotler and Turner (1995) *Marketing Management*, 8th edn. Scarborough, Ontario: Prentice Hall.

KPMG Management Consulting (1992) *Investment Networking.* Glasgow: Scottish Enterprise.

Landstrom, H. (1995) "The relationship between private investors and small firms: an agency theory approach", *Entrepreneurship and Regional Development*, vol. 4, pp. 199–223.

Maier, J. and Walker, D. (1987) "The role of venture capital in financing small business", *Journal of Business Venturing*, vol. 1, pp. 207–14.

Mason, C. and Harrison, R. (1991) "A strategy for closing the small firm equity gap", *Venture Finance Research Working Paper No. 3*, University of Southampton and University of Ulster.

Mason, C. and Harrison, R. (1993) "Strategies for expanding the informal venture capital market", *International Small Business Journal*, vol. II, no. 4, pp. 23–38.

Mason, C. and Harrison, R. (1994a) "The informal venture capital market in the UK", in Hughes, A. and Storey, D. (eds), *Financing Small Firms*. London: Routledge, pp. 64–111.

Mason, C. and Harrison, R. (1994b) "Why Business Angels say no: a case study of opportunities rejected by an informal investor syndicate", *Venture Finance Research Project Working Paper No. 7*, University of Southampton and University of Ulster.

Mason, C. and Harrison, R. (1995) "Informal venture capital and the financing of small and medium-sized enterprises", *Small Enterprise Research—The Journal of SEAANZ*, vol. 3, nos 1 and 2, pp. 33–56.

Mason, C. and Harrison, R. (1996) "The UK clearing banks and the informal venture capital market", *International Journal of Bank Marketing*, vol. 14, no. 1, pp. 5–14.

Mason, C., Harrison, R. and Allen, P. (1995) "Informal venture capital: a study of the investment process, the post-investment experience and investment performance", *Venture Finance Research Project Working Paper No. 12.*

Mason, C., Harrison, R. and Chaloner, J. (1991a) "The operation and effectiveness of LINC, part 1: a survey of investors", *Urban Policy Research Unit Working Paper*, University of Southampton and Ulster Business School.

Mason, C., Harrison, R. and Chaloner, J. (1991b) "The informal risk capital market in the UK: a study of the investor characteristics, investment preferences and investment decision-making", *Venture Finance Working Paper No. 2,* University of Southampton and University of Ulster.

Mason, C. and Rogers, A. (1996) "Understanding the business angel's investment decision", *Venture Finance Research Project, Working Paper No. 14*, University of Southampton and University of Ulster.

Moore, G. (1995) *Inside the Tornado*. New York: Harper Business Press.

Moore, K. and Andradi, B. (1996) "Who will be the big winners on the Internet?", *Journal of Brand Management*, Fall.

Murray, G. (1994) "Evolution and change: analysis of the first decade of the UK venture capital industry", cited in Mason, C. and Harrison, R., "Why Business Angels say no: a case study of opportunities rejected by an informal investor syndicate", *Venture Finance Research Project Working Paper No. 7*, University of Southampton and University of Ulster.

National Westminster Bank (1993) "Extracts from a study into private investor networks". Research commissioned by National Westminster Bank plc Technology Unit and carried out by The Innovation Partnership, Manchester.

Oates, D. (1992) "Visions of Angels", *Director*, June, pp. 35–38 and 80.

Oswald, S. and Boulton, W. (1995) "Obtaining industry control: the case of the pharmaceutical distribution industry", *California Management Review*, Fall.

Peek, J. and Rosengren, E. (1992) "The capital crunch in New England", *New England Economic Review*, May/June, pp. 21–31.

Pine, J. (1997) *Mass Customization: The New Frontier in Business Competition.* Boston, MA: Harvard Business School Press.

Porter, M. (1980) *Competitive Strategy*. London: Free Press.

Porter, M. (1983) "End game strategies for declining industries", *Harvard Business Review*, July–August, pp. 111–20.

Riding, A., Dal Cin, P., Duxbury, L., Haines, G. and Safrata, R. (1993) *Informal Investors in Canada: The Identification of Salient Characteristics*. Ottawa: Carleton University.

Robinson, R. (1987) "Emerging strategies in the venture capital industry", *Journal of Business Venturing*, vol. 2, pp. 53–77.

Rogers, E. (1995) *Adoption of Innovations*, 4th edn. London: Free Press.

Smith, D. (1994) "The financing gap that taxes the minds of ministers", *Management Today*, August, pp. 15–18.

Stanworth, J., Purdy, D. and Kirby, D. (1992) "The management of success in 'growth corridor' small firms", cited in CBI (1993) "Finance for growth: meeting the financing needs of small and medium enterprises", *A Report of the Confederation of British Industry (CBI) Smaller Firms Council*. London: CBI.

Sterne, J. (1996) *Customer Service on the Internet*. New York: John Wiley.

Stevenson, H. and Coveney, P. (1994) *Survey of Business Angels: Fallacies Corrected and Six Distinct Types of Angel Identified*. Henley-on-Thames: Venture Capital Report.

Sullivan, M. and Miller, A. (1990) "Applying theory of finance to informal risk capital research: promise and problems", in Churchill, N., Bygrave, W., Hornaday, J., Vesper, K. and Wetzel, W. (eds), *Frontiers of Entrepreneurship Research*. Wellesley, MA: Babson College, pp. 296–310.

Sweeting, R. (1991) "UK venture capital funds and the funding of new technology-based businesses: process and relationships", *Journal of Management Studies*, vol. 28, pp. 601–22.

van Osnabrugge, M. (1998) "The financing of entrepreneurial firms in the UK: a comparison of Business Angel and venture capitalist investment resources", Unpublished doctoral thesis, Oxford University.

Wetzel, W. (1983) "Angels and informal risk capital", *Sloan Management Review*, Summer, pp. 23–34.

Wetzel, W. (1987) "The informal risk capital market: aspects of scale and efficiency", *Journal of Business Venturing*, vol. 2, pp. 299–313.

Wetzel, W. and Freear, J. (1993) "Promoting informal venture capital in the United States: reflections on the history of VCN", in Harrison, R. and Mason, C. (eds), *Informal Venture Capital: Information, Networks and Public Policy*. Hemel Hempstead: Woodhead-Faulkner.

Woolfman, G. (ed.) (1993) *A Summary of the Current Investment Preferences of the UK Venture Capital Industry with a Brief Look at Trends*. Levy Lee, Chartered Accountants.

Yip, G. (1995) *Total Global Strategy*, Englewood Cliffs, NJ: Prentice Hall.

Index

Note: page numbers in *italic* refer to tables or figures.

*Index compiled by Liz Granger
– Indexing Services*